Institute of Leadership
& Management

Working with Costs and Budgets

FIFTH EDITION

Published for the
Institute of Leadership & Management

ELSEVIER

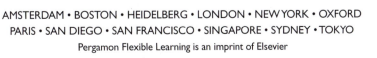

AMSTERDAM · BOSTON · HEIDELBERG · LONDON · NEW YORK · OXFORD
PARIS · SAN DIEGO · SAN FRANCISCO · SINGAPORE · SYDNEY · TOKYO
Pergamon Flexible Learning is an imprint of Elsevier

Pergamon
Flexible
Learning

Pergamon Flexible Learning is an imprint of Elsevier
Linacre House, Jordan Hill, Oxford OX2 8DP, UK
30 Corporate Drive, Suite 400, Burlington, MA 01803, USA

First edition 1986
Second edition 1991
Third edition 1997
Fourth edition 2003
Fifth edition 2007

Editor: David Pardey

Based on material in previous editions of this work

The views expressed in this work are those of the authors and do
not necessarily reflect those of the Institute of Leadership &
Management or of the publisher

Notice
No responsibility is assumed by the publisher for any injury and/or damage to persons or
property as a matter of products liability, negligence or otherwise, or from any use or operation
of any methods, products, instructions or ideas contained in the material herein

British Library Cataloguing in Publication Data
A catalogue record for this book is available from the British Library

Library of Congress Cataloguing in Publication Data
A catalogue record for this book is available from the Library of Congress

ISBN 978-0-08-046430-5

For information on all Pergamon Flexible Learning publications
visit our website at http://books.elsevier.com

Institute of Leadership & Management
Registered Office
1 Giltspur Street
London
EC1A 9DD
Telephone: 020 7294 2470
www.i-l-m.com
ILM is a part of the City & Guilds Group

Typeset by Charon Tec Ltd (A Macmillan Company), Chennai, India
www.charontec.com
Printed and bound in Great Britain

07 08 09 10 11   10 9 8 7 6 5 4 3 2 1

Contents

Contents

Series preface

Whether you are a tutor/trainer or studying management development to further your career, Super Series provides an exciting and flexible resource to help you to achieve your goals. The fifth edition is completely new and up-to-date, and has been structured to perfectly match the Institute of Leadership & Management (ILM)'s new unit-based qualifications for first line managers. It also harmonizes with the 2004 national occupational standards in management and leadership, providing an invaluable resource for S/NVQs at Level 3 in Management.

Super Series is equally valuable for anyone tutoring or studying any management programmes at this level, whether leading to a qualification or not. Individual workbooks also support short programmes, which may be recognized by ILM as Endorsed or Development Awards, or provide the ideal way to undertake CPD activities.

For learners, coping with all the pressures of today's world, Super Series offers you the flexibility to study at your own pace to fit around your professional and other commitments. You don't need a PC or to attend classes at a specific time – choose when and where to study to suit yourself! And you will always have the complete workbook as a quick reference just when you need it.

For tutors/trainers, Super Series provides an invaluable guide to what needs to be covered, and in what depth. It also allows learners who miss occasional sessions to 'catch up' by dipping into the series.

Super Series provides unrivalled support for all those involved in first line management and supervision.

Unit specification

Title:	Working with costs and budgets		Unit Ref:	M3.27
Level:	3			
Credit value:	I			

Learning outcomes *The learner* will	Assessment criteria *The learner can (in an organization with which the learner is familiar)*	
I. Know how to work to a budget	I.I	Explain the importance of agreeing to a budget and operating within it
	I.2	Describe a method to monitor variance between actual performance and budget
	I.3	Explain how information used in determining and/or revising budgets is gathered
2. Understand costs	2.I	Explain fixed and variable costs; and the concept of break even in relation to the organization
	2.2	Explain the purpose and nature of basic cost statements
	2.3	Explain the value of standard costing and its role as a control mechanism
	2.4	Briefly describe mechanisms in the organization to maintain control of costs

Workbook introduction

 ## 1 ILM Super Series study links

This workbook addresses the issues of *Costs and Budgets*. Should you wish to extend your study to other Super Series workbooks covering related or different subject areas, you will find a comprehensive list at the back of this book.

 ## 2 Links to ILM qualifications

This workbook relates to the learning outcomes of Unit M3.27 Working with costs and budgets from the ILM Level 3 Award, Certificate and Diploma in First Line Management.

3 Links to S/NVQs in Management

This workbook relates to the following Units of the Management Standards which are used in S/NVQs in Management, as well as a range of other S/NVQs:

D6. Allocate and monitor the progress and quality of work in your area of responsibility

4 Workbook objectives

In our daily lives we all need to control expenditure (another name for costs), so that we have money to spend and save. Companies also need to control costs to help them make a profit and reinvest for the future. Business organizations must be competitive to survive, so keeping costs under control is an essential activity. Other organizations need to control costs to make the best use of resources.

We need to distinguish between cost control and cost reduction. Cost reduction is usually undertaken as a systematic programme to reduce existing levels of costs, perhaps because a company is facing difficulties, or needs to be able to match the prices of competitors. It may involve changing working methods, new sources of supply, or employing fewer people.

Cost control is a continuous and routine management function. It is almost certainly part of your job, for costs aren't just the concern of accountants and senior managers. What's more, you and your work team contribute to the final cost of whatever goods or services you provide, so it is important that you take an active interest in cost control.

In this workbook we will look at ways of controlling and monitoring costs. You will improve your understanding of these matters so that you and your work team can be more effective. And because most events and activities cost money, you will know that it's usually necessary to make financial plans to achieve your aims.

The same principles are relevant at work. Your organization has aims and objectives with financial implications and these are identified by using budgets.

By preparing budgets which allocate money to specific purposes, an organization seeks to gain more control over its activities. Careful monitoring then helps to ensure that spending is kept within bounds. Budgets are considered an essential tool by organizations in the management of their affairs.

Throughout the workbook we look at examples from different organizations. Some may or may not be directly relevant to you at the moment, but the principles may be appropriate to something you do at work. Costing techniques were developed for practical purposes. You should use them when relevant and not when they would be too costly to use or of little benefit. Of course, this means that you must be aware of what is available to you. Remember that there is value in a breadth of knowledge, even where something does not immediately appear relevant to you.

4.1 Objectives

When you have completed this workbook you will be better able to:

- identify different costs and how they behave;
- appreciate how important it is to control costs;
- understand how standard costing techniques help to control costs;
- use different methods for controlling and reducing costs;
- understand what a budget is and how they are used;
- help to draw up workable budgets;
- use some budgetary control techniques.

5 Activity planner

The following Activities need some planning and you may want to look at them now.

Activity 10   Here you are being asked to think about obtaining 'value for money' from your work team and you may like to think about this as you study your workbook before reaching that activity.

Activity 13   Here you are being asked to think about breakdowns in production or delivery of service and ways in which you could counteract these problems.

Activity 34   You are invited to consider how to communicate the need for cost consciousness to your work team.

Activity 41   You are asked to consider any occasions where you have had to control resources.

Activity 48   You are asked to consider which aspects of your budget are in and outside your control.

Activity 51   You are asked about reporting budget variances.

Some or all of these Activities may provide the basis of evidence for your S/NVQ portfolio. All Portfolio Activities and the Work-based assignment (on page 111) are sign-posted with this icon:

This icon will always show the unit to which the activity or Work-based assignment relates.

Note that the Work-based assignment suggests that you speak to your manager, finance director or to your colleagues in the accounts office about the way in which costs are controlled in your organization.

You might like to start thinking now about who to approach and arrange to speak with them.

Session A
Classifying costs

1 Introduction

At home, if your expenses or costs are high in comparison to your income, your life can be difficult. Say, for example, that the electricity, gas and telephone bills are all due at the same time and your wages are only enough to pay two of them. What do you do?

Let's assume you negotiate time to pay but realize that the same problem is likely to occur next quarter. You'll have to decide whether to turn down the heating, switch off the lights or cut back on phone calls.

Businesses can find themselves in similar situations. It is up to you and everyone in your organization to be concerned about the costs of whatever you produce or supply, just as you should be concerned about quality.

Business organizations in the private sector who do not control costs may go out of business. Organizations in the public sector with high and increasing costs will need to make severe cuts in their activities and will attract a great deal of criticism from the public and government of the day. As a first line manager, you'll need to be concerned with costs and their control.

In this session we will look at the different kinds of cost and how you can help to control them.

2 Organizational costs

The **total costs** of an organization are made up of such things as:

- wages and salaries;
- electricity, gas and other utilities;
- purchase of steel, wood, stationery, X-ray plates or whatever raw materials the organization uses;
- payments for services from transport to cleaning.

These costs are deducted from the **sales** of the organization; the difference is **profit**. Profit might also be called operating surplus by organizations in the public and voluntary sectors.

Sales (or income) – Costs = Profit (or operating surplus)

Several ways of setting prices are based on the idea of determining costs and then adding a percentage for profit. Identifying costs is, therefore, important.

The implication of this is that an organization can either **increase its prices** or **decrease its costs** to become more profitable or to alter the level of its operating surplus.

But, there are dangers with these courses of action.

Activity 1

3 mins

Suppose the price of your favourite biscuits was suddenly doubled.

Jot down **three** things you might do.

_____

_____

_____

_____

EXTENSION 1
You can explore the relationship of costs and pricing further in Kirkland's and Howard's book *Simple and Practical Costing, Pricing and Credit Control*.

You might:

- buy fewer biscuits;
- stop buying the biscuits;
- buy biscuits made by a competitor;
- buy an alternative product, such as cake;
- cut back on something else so you could afford the biscuits.

People who buy your organization's products may choose one of these options if you increase your prices. You probably don't have much to do with fixing selling prices, but you **are** in a position to affect costs. By controlling these you can help your organization, and that's what we'll concentrate on.

As a first line manager you will be concerned with the following costs:

- labour costs;
- materials costs;
- overheads.

3 Labour costs

The total 'labour cost' of employing people in the organization comprises the wages or salaries that they receive directly, plus the additional costs to the employer of National Insurance contributions, pension contributions and other benefits. It depends on the type of organization, but the costs of labour are often the most significant cost of all.

If the organization makes something that is sold or supplied, then its total labour cost is often split into direct and indirect labour costs.

Wages that can be identified with a particular product are usually called **direct labour costs**. Some examples of direct labour are:

- painting a product;
- welding a part;
- sewing a garment;
- dealing with customers;
- processing data;
- a hairdresser doing a cut and blow dry.

Wages that cannot be identified with a particular product are **indirect labour costs**. Examples of indirect labour can arise from a number of activities, such as:

- maintenance costs;
- cleaning;
- employing a salesforce;
- operating a marketing department.

None of these can be identified directly with a particular item of production, even though they are essential for an organization as a whole.

Direct labour costs will increase or decrease in proportion to the production activity being carried out and for this reason are called **variable costs**.

Indirect labour costs happen all the time, whether something is being produced or not. They are **fixed costs**.

We will look at the significance of fixed and variable costs a little later on.

4 Materials costs

In manufacturing, materials costs can often account for more than half of the total costs of production.

In industries such as aero-engineering and computer manufacturing, you can appreciate that the costs of materials such as steel, plastic and microchips will probably make up much of the total costs of the finished product. Conversely, a telephone banking operation or call centre may find that materials costs account for much less than one tenth of total costs.

We already know that labour costs can be broken down into direct and indirect categories. Materials costs can also be divided into:

- direct materials costs;
- indirect materials costs.

Direct materials costs are the costs of materials used in the products, such as:

- wood;
- steel;
- paper;
- component parts;
- ingredients for meals;
- plant food and compost.

Direct materials costs can be identified directly and in total with an item being produced.

Indirect materials costs are the costs of such materials as:

- cleaning products;
- paper and stationery;
- lubricants.

Indirect materials costs CANNOT be identified directly and in total with an item being produced.

If a material is used for different jobs, it may not be possible to identify all the costs as either direct or indirect. Let's look at an example.

Suppose you work for an organization which makes a range of timber products. One of the items is garden sheds, which are all painted. The same paint is used to decorate the factory premises.

Activity 2 · 2 mins

Complete the statements below with a suitable word or words.

■ The paint used on the factory is _____ _____ materials cost.

■ The paint used on the garden sheds is _____ _____ materials cost.

The paint used on the factory premises is **an indirect** materials cost, because it cannot be identified in total or directly with the making of sheds.

The paint used on the garden sheds is **a direct** materials cost, because it can be identified in total and directly with the making of sheds.

5 Overheads

Costs that are incurred but that are not easily identified with any particular process or product are called **overheads**. General overheads include:

■ insurance of stocks of materials and finished goods, machinery and people;
■ heating and lighting;
■ rates.

We have already seen two other types of overhead. Wages of people not directly involved in production or directly providing a service (indirect labour) are classed as labour overheads. Examples are:

- security staff;
- maintenance fitters;
- managers and supervisors;
- secretaries and reception staff.

Indirect materials are materials overheads: safety clothing and cleaning materials are examples.

Activity 3 · 2 mins

Which of the following are direct and which indirect material or labour costs?

	Direct	Indirect
1 Materials used to make a particular product or provide a service.	☐	☐
2 Wages of work teams whose time is spent entirely on manufacturing or service provision.	☐	☐
3 Receptionist's salary.	☐	☐

Materials used in these ways are **direct** materials costs, and the wages of work teams whose time is spent entirely on manufacturing or service provision are **direct** labour costs. The receptionist's salary is an **indirect** labour cost or labour **overhead**.

Now let's complete our examination of cost headings with how we can collect together types of materials, labour and general overheads.

- Factory or operations overheads.

These include general overheads, such as factory or operations centre heating, lighting, rent and rates; labour overheads, such as supervisory and reception staff; and materials overheads, such as stationery, safety clothing and cleaning materials.

■ Selling and distribution overheads.

These include general overheads such as sales office and despatch centre heating and lighting, advertising and catalogues and maintenance of cars and lorries, and labour overheads, such as sales staff commission and expenses.

■ Administration overheads.

These include accounting and financial costs, the hire of and depreciation of computers, office supplies and stationery, maintenance and depreciation of the building and its contents. They comprise a mix of materials, labour and general overheads.

Manufacturing organizations **make** things. But retail organizations are in the business of buying and selling – **trading** in other words. Insurance companies, chartered accountants and surveyors do not sell goods in any form. They sell a **service** that doesn't involve any processing of materials or selling of goods. Let's look at cost headings in such organizations.

Activity 4   3 mins

Tick the relevant boxes for each classification of cost that you would expect to find in a retail organization and a service organization, respectively.

Classification of cost	Retailer	Service organization
Direct labour		
Direct materials, or goods for resale		
Shop or operations overheads		
Selling and distribution overheads		
Administration overheads		

You probably felt quite confident in ticking all three categories of overhead for both types of organization, and the goods for resale category for the retailer. But does either organization have direct labour, and does the service organization have direct materials? The answer is: yes, if they choose to do so. In other words, an organization can choose whether or not to classify items as direct or indirect, operational or overheads, depending on what it wants to achieve with its cost classifications. We shall come back to this important idea later.

Let's look first at another important way of classifying costs, not by means of their element but by their behaviour.

6 Fixed and variable costs

You will remember that we have already said that costs which vary with output are called **variable costs**. Costs which don't are called **fixed costs**.

Let's look at an example of each.

■   Variable cost

A baker sells bread in paper bags and cakes in boxes. The packaging material is directly related to the output of bread and cakes and is a **variable** cost.

■   Fixed cost

The monthly repayments of a mortgage on the baker's shop is not affected in any way by how much bread or how many cakes are sold, so this is a **fixed** cost. That doesn't necessarily mean that fixed costs don't change. Mortgage repayments can change, because interest rates change, but the reasons for the change are not related to the output of bread and cakes.

EXTENSION I
Sometimes fixed costs can be converted to variable costs. Take a look at Kirkland's and Howard's book *Simple and Practical Costing, Pricing and Credit Control* which illustrates how this works.

Often, production wages are variable as they vary with output. If a hospital increases the number of patients treated, more nurses have to be taken on or extra overtime paid. Variable costs need not vary **exactly** in proportion to output or service provision. If a sudden drop in demand occurs, it's unlikely that people would immediately be laid off.

Activity 5 ·

June Hamilton manages one of a chain of small shops. Some of the costs incurred by her shop are listed below. Some of these costs vary, depending on the amount of business June's shop does, and some stay the same, regardless of how well the business is doing.

Tick the appropriate boxes to identify costs which vary and which remain the same.

	Varies	Stays the same
Rent	☐	☐
Rates	☐	☐
Wages of sales staff	☐	☐
Wages of part-time bookkeeper	☐	☐
Commission on sales	☐	☐
Packaging material	☐	☐
Electricity for lighting and heating	☐	☐
Insurance of the property and the stock	☐	☐

I would say that rent, rates, electricity and insurance would stay the same, regardless of the amount of business June's shop does. Commission on sales and packaging materials vary depending on how much is sold. Wages stay the same in the short term but can be varied if business improves or worsens dramatically.

Costs which remain the same whether the level of business activity rises or falls are called **fixed costs**.

Costs which vary with changes in the amount of business beings done are called **variable costs**.

Distinguishing between fixed and variable costs can sometimes be quite a complex issue as we have seen in the case of wages.

Now that you've examined elements of costs and how they can be classified into separate headings which may, or may not, vary with the level of activity in the workplace, we're ready to start examining ways in which we can use this information.

7 Break-even analysis

A simple technique called **break-even analysis** is widely used by all kinds of organizations. It allows an organization to see the minimum level of operations it must maintain to at least cover its fixed costs – its **break-even point**.

This determines the level of production and sales a business needs to break even – that is, to make no profit but no loss.

Every unit produced and sold above break-even results in profit.	Every unit produced and sold below break-even results in a loss.

To use break-even analysis to plan operations, we have to classify all costs, as we have already done, into **fixed costs** and **variable costs**.

For instance, a shop might be looking at whether it can continue in business over the summer period. All its staff have to be given at least one month's notice of dismissal. For the three month period, therefore, it would be best to treat wages as a fixed cost.

Let's see how it would work.

> Unique Double Glazing expects to sell 1,000 window units at £200 each.
>
> It expects fixed costs (rates, management salaries, machine maintenance, etc.) to be £50,000. Variable costs (materials, direct wages etc.) per window are £100 per unit.

We can anticipate the following.

- Each window unit sold adds £200 to income but £100 to costs (the £50,000 fixed costs will exist no matter what the level of sales). The £100 surplus on each window unit sold is called **contribution per unit**.

- When the contribution from each window unit sold matches the fixed cost, the break-even point, at which Unique makes no profit and no loss, has been reached.

In our example, we have the following:

fixed costs $= £50,000$

contribution per unit $= £100$

$$\text{break-even point} = \frac{£50,000}{£100} = 500 \text{ units}$$

If the company sells 500 units, which is 50 per cent of its target, it will have broken even. If it sells more, it will make a profit: if it sells fewer, it will make a loss.

Remember, the company expects to sell 1,000 units, and profit equals sales minus costs (both fixed and variable).

Activity 6 · 5 mins

Calculate the business target profit for Unique Double Glazing if expected sales are achieved.

_____

_____

_____

_____

_____

_____

I hope your calculations worked out something like this.

Sales	1,000 × £200		£200,000
Less: Variable costs	1,000 × £100	£100,000	
Fixed costs		£50,000	(£150,000)
Profit			£50,000

We can also express this as:

500 units above break-even × £100 (contribution) = £50,000.

Activity 7

6 mins

What will be the position if Unique Double Glazing sells:

a 600 units?

_____

_____

_____

b 400 units?

_____

_____

_____

a If the business sells 600 units, that is 100 units more than the break-even point. The profit will then be 100 × £100 = £10,000 profit.

b If sales only reach 400 units, that is 100 units below break-even, and the business will make a loss of 100 × £100 = £10,000 loss.

Break-even analysis is useful in helping to:

■ decide what price to charge to easily meet the break-even point and make a profit;
■ decide whether to make something yourself or to buy it in;
■ decide whether to close-down (whether to stop producing goods, provide services and so on, which do not break even).

These are major decisions, and not necessarily ones in which first line managers will become involved. We shall look at them in Session C.

So how is break-even analysis useful in practice? Well, it helps to focus the minds of everyone in the organization on the need to control costs (and generate income).

For instance, you might be manager of a newsagent, with staff costs per hour of £20. You sell *The Times* newspaper at 40p per copy. This means you have to sell 50 copies of *The Times* per hour to break even, assuming you sell nothing else and have no other costs (£20/40p). In practice, of course, you would have had to buy your stock of *The Times* from a wholesaler, so reducing the amount you make on the sale. You can see that a quiet hour or day, therefore, is money pouring down the drain.

Activity 8

Identify how much it costs your organization to employ you by the hour by calculating your hourly wage rate and adding about 10% for National Insurance.

If you work in a commercial organization, work out your organization's break-even point for you in terms of sales of one of your products.

If you work in a non-profit organization, work out how much extra funding is needed so that the organization continues to make neither a profit nor a loss.

Make your notes on a separate sheet of paper.

You may find it useful from now on to think of the effects on the break-even point for your workplace of any increase in how much it pays you and how hard you work.

8 The need to control costs

It's sometimes difficult to decide which costs are fixed and which variable. In the longer term, virtually nothing is fixed. We usually regard business rates, for example, as a fixed cost as they are a payment demanded by the local authority, and outside the control of the business. But rates vary between one town and another, and may increase or decrease from year to year. A business can reduce its rates bill. It can move!

Fixed costs are fixed over a period of time, and that timescale is linked to the scale of decision making that takes place in the organization. For instance, a power generator has to make very long-term plans. It is not easy to move a power station! But the situation for an employment agency is far more fluid. On a day-to-day level, the important distinction we have to make is between the costs we can control and those we cannot.

Activity 9 · ⏱ 2 mins

Tick the costs below that you think you can influence at work.

Large airlines use a 'hub and spoke' model to spread high fixed servicing costs over many aircraft. All flights go to a hub airport where there are flights to hundreds of possible final destinations (spokes).

■ Quarterly electricity cost. ☐

■ Rent of the firm's premises. ☐

■ Rental cost of each telephone line. ☐

■ Quarterly cost of telephone calls. ☐

The cost of electricity and telephone calls made can be kept down by your own efforts.

Perhaps you feel, particularly if you work for a large organization, that the amount of electricity you use or how many telephone calls you make doesn't make any real difference on the overall total.

To some extent you're right. If you turn off lights when you go out of a room or make a shorter telephone call it will make a difference of only a few pounds a quarter. But by setting an example to your work team you can encourage your team members to control costs. You will also exert quite a bit of influence on other people who come into your work area, if they see that you take cost control seriously.

As a general rule, variable costs are more likely to be within your control than fixed costs, and it is these which you can most easily help to keep down by your own efforts.

What can we do about other costs which are not directly within the control of the people involved?

Let's take an example of your work team's time. How much they are paid and their pay scale is probably outside your control. But you can make sure that value for money is obtained for that cost.

Activity 10 · 10 mins

S/NVQ
D6

This Activity may provide the basis of evidence for your S/NVQ portfolio. If you are intending to take this course of action, it might be better to write your answers on separate sheets of paper.

Jot down **one** way in which you can ensure that you get 'value for money' for the cost of your work team's time. Make a note of ways in which you can implement your suggestion.

_____

_____

_____

Perhaps you said something like 'keep them working', or 'make efficient use of their time', or even 'manage them properly'. You may have started to think in detail about selecting the right people for the job and training them properly. Perhaps you could draw up a time schedule for yourself and your team.

Now look at this example.

Activity 11 · 2 mins

Shari's work team uses computer screens which are linked to a large computer at head office. Frequently they spend long, frustrating periods in front of the screen waiting for responses from the heavily loaded computer. Response time is slow and seems to be getting worse. She is able to use her work team's time on other jobs so that their time isn't wasted so much, but the real problem doesn't go away. What can she do?

Write down one suggestion.

_____

_____

_____

_____

She could try a number of possibilities, for example:

- ring head office and try to find out what the problem is;
- talk to her manager about it and get him or her to take it up.

If Shari was to report 'a general feeling' that response time is getting worse, it may not meet with much reaction. It would be more helpful if she kept a record of the problems and noted exactly what was happening.

In any situation, and equipped with some real evidence, you can:

- identify the scale of the problem yourself;
- convince your manager that you have a problem which you cannot solve on your own.

We'll look at this in detail later in the workbook.

To sum up, we can say that you can tackle problems of costs on three fronts:

- keep down costs which are within your control;
- get value for money for costs which you can't control directly;
- keep records of cost problems which you have identified but can't influence without support.

Self-assessment 1

10 mins

1 Identify the differences between direct and indirect materials costs.

_____

_____

_____

2   Claire runs a local newspaper. She pays her advertising sales staff on a commission-only basis and her reporters are given a weekly wage. Are the different forms of wage fixed or variable costs?

■ the wages of the advertising sales staff are _____ _____;

■ the wages of the reporters are _____ _____.

3   Fill in the missing words in the following sentences.

a Direct labour costs _____ be _____ identified with a particular product.

b Wages which _____ be identified with a particular product are _____ labour costs.

c Direct labour costs are often _____ costs because they increase or decrease in proportion to the production being carried out.

4   The Feelgood Health Club has weekly fixed costs of £18,000 per week. There are no variable costs. Each member pays £15 per week to be a member. What is Feelgood's break-even number of members?

5   Sam is a first line manager in a factory assembling PCs. Tick the costs which would be under Sam's control and those which would not.

	Controllable	Not controllable
■ wastage of components used in the production of PCs	☐	☐
■ advertising costs of PCs	☐	☐
■ Sam's basic salary	☐	☐

Answers to these questions can be found on page 121.

9 Summary

- Profit = Sales – Costs.

- Costs are broadly made up of **labour costs**, **materials costs** and **overheads**.

- Labour costs have to be divided into:

  - direct labour costs – which can be totally identified with time spent making a particular product or proving a service;
  - indirect labour costs – which are identified with work other than making a product or directly providing a service.

- Materials costs, like labour costs, have to be divided into direct and indirect materials costs.

- Costs that relate to supporting the main activity are called overheads. Overheads can include indirect materials and labour, depending on how the organization classifies its costs.

- Costs can be identified as:

  - **variable** – varying with output;
  - **fixed** – incurred regardless of output.

- Each unit an organization sells makes a contribution to fixed costs of its selling price less its variable costs of production. An organization breaks even when its fixed costs are covered by its total contribution. If it sells more it makes a profit; if it sells less it makes a loss.

- The break-even point, at which an organization makes neither a profit nor a loss, is calculated as fixed costs/contribution per unit.

- To control costs:

  - continually monitor and minimize costs within your control;
  - get value for money from costs you cannot directly control;
  - keep records of costs you cannot control without support.

Session B
Standard costing

1 Introduction

You know that it is useful to control costs. But how do you know you are controlling the right ones? And by how much should you reduce them, if possible? You can switch lights off and turn down the heating, but your work team are unlikely to work well in the cold and dark.

It helps you to control anything – the output of a machine or a work team, for instance – if there is a standard against which to measure performance.

In cost control, the first step is to decide what the costs should be and then control what happens in such a way that you meet those 'target' costs. If actual costs of the operation turn out to be different from the expected figure, then you look at the differences – called variances – and find out why they are different. Then you can decide what action should be taken to bring them back to target.

In this session we will look at different standards and how to use them to control costs.

2 Setting standards

Standard costs are concerned with individual units of production or service. Each item of production or service, for instance, will have a standard cost.

A standard cost is a predetermined cost that is achieved by setting standards related to particular circumstances or conditions of work.

> Costs change over time, so standards should be reviewed regularly to ensure that they are still relevant.

A standard cost should indicate not just what a particular cost is **expected** to be, but also what it **ought** to be under certain conditions.

You can apply standard costs to all the costs in the workplace. These may include:

- direct labour;
- direct materials;
- overheads (fixed and variable).

A mechanic may, for example, be expected to complete the servicing of a car in an hour and this will involve one hour's direct labour cost plus a direct materials cost for, say, oil filter, lubricants and other replacement parts.

2.1 Standard cost rates

Standard cost rates are estimated by taking all sorts of considerations into account.

Activity 12 · 5 mins

a Jot down **two** things which you would take into account in estimating materials costs for something which will be used extensively in your work-place for the next year.

_____

_____

b Write down **two** matters you would have to take into account in estimating labour costs for a forthcoming period.

_____

_____

I hope you have thought of taking the following into account in respect of materials costs:

- the purchase price;
- any expected change in price (for instance, you might know that the price of oil or floppy disks was going to increase);
- any discount you could negotiate.

The following factors, among others, would be relevant for labour costs:

- the current hourly rate/piece rate;
- likely agreements on pay rises;
- other costs, such as overtime premiums, bonuses, employer's National Insurance contributions, pension contributions.

Deciding on how much things ought to cost is only one side of the question. The other matter to consider is how many of the things in question should be used for each unit of production or service. In other words, we need to decide how well production will perform.

So now let's look at performance standard rates.

2.2 Standard performance rates

To use a standard costing system, somebody must decide:

- the quantities, types and mix of materials to produce any given product;
- the amount and type of labour to produce any given product or service.

These technical standards are usually set by specialists and involve techniques such as method study and job evaluation.

Two types of standard are commonly used:

- ideal standards;
- expected standards.

Ideal standards are based on perfect working conditions. However, conditions are seldom perfect, often for reasons outside our immediate control. Ideal standards can help to highlight major variances, but people tend to find them rather discouraging, because the targets may be too high.

Much better, usually, are **expected standards**. These could well be called realistic standards, as they build in an allowance for an acceptable level of inefficiency. If the work team is well managed and willing to co-operate, expected standards should be attainable.

Activity 13

5 mins

S/NVQ
D6

This Activity may provide the basis of appropriate evidence for your S/NVQ portfolio. If you are intending to take this course of action, it might be better to write your answers on separate sheets of paper.

Identify three causes for breaks in production or delivery of service which are not planned and which your work team has experienced. Suggest changes that you could recommend to your manager to address such situations.

_____

_____

_____

_____

_____

_____

_____

Certain planned breaks are important to allow staff to eat and rest physically and mentally. They are often required by law, say in the case of lorry drivers and users of VDUs. There are, though, breaks that can occur unexpectedly, such as:

■ when equipment breaks down. A hairdresser may have spare cutting equipment to call upon but if a baker's oven breaks down, replacement may not be possible. A rapid service and repair contract is essential.

■ where the organization runs out of stock and production ceases. Plans for alternative work so that employees have something to do would avoid unnecessary costs, or alternative stockholding policies could be employed.

■ when accidents or injuries occur. Good health and safety training and procedures should limit this problem.

2.3 Standard costing and non-manufacturing organizations

A full standard costing system is less common in organizations that provide a service rather than manufacture something. Many industries, nevertheless, find it useful to set performance standards in order to:

a   base costs upon them, and then;
b   measure actual performance.

For example, a building contractor might base costs on performance standards for:

■ cubic metres of earth excavated per hour by a mechanical digger;

■ lorry loads of earth shifted per day;

■ bricks laid per hour.

Activity 14

3 mins

In an office you may find sales order processing clerks, and administrators sending letters in response to queries at work. Also the manager may spend a lot of time talking to clients in a separate office.

Suggest two possible performance standards which you could set if you were in charge in this situation.

You could set performance standards for:

■ letters created per hour by an administrator;

■ percentage completion of correct invoices by the sales order processing clerks;

■ number of deals by the manager per day.

3 Standard costing in practice

Let's look first at a very simple example.

Karl makes large, luxury cages for pet rats. He knows that each cage requires 6 square metres of wire mesh, and 12 metres of timber. It takes him 3.5 hours to make a cage. Wire mesh costs £2 per square metre, and timber costs £1.50 per metre. He pays himself £15 per hour. What is the standard cost for each cage?

We can calculate this by drawing up a standard cost statement. Make sure you can trace every item in the figure below to the information above, and that you can follow through the calculations.

Standard cost statement: Rat cage

		Quantity used	Rate £	Standard cost £
Direct materials				
	Wire mesh	6	2.00	12.00
	Timber	12	1.50	18.00
Direct labour				
	Karl's time	3.5	15.00	52.50
Standard cost per cage				82.50

Once you are happy that you understand the way in which this standard cost statement is constructed, you can put standard costing into operation in the following Activity.

Activity 15

5 mins

Plastiform plc makes a range of plastic furniture. A standard costing system is in operation. The following information is available for one product – plastic tables.

The raw material (plastic) has been costed at £6.10 per metre. The standard usage of material is reckoned to be 5 metres per table.

Two types of labour are required in the production process: moulders and cutters.

- The standard rate for moulders is £8.00 per hour.
- The standard rate for cutters is £10.00 per hour.
- The expected standard for moulders is 1½ hours per table.
- The expected standard for cutters is 2½ hours per table.

Complete the standard cost statement below to show what the standard cost will be for a table.

> **Standard cost statement: plastic table**
>
> Direct materials: 5 metres at £6.10   = £ _____
>
> Direct wages:
>
> Moulder _____ hours × £ _____   = £6.00
>
> Cutter   _____ hours × £ _____   = _____
>
>   _____

The answer to this Activity can be found on page 124.

The system an organization uses to analyse and ultimately to control its costs can be as simple or as complicated as the organization wishes. Karl and Plastiform plc produce standard cost statements just for direct materials and labour. What about overheads?

We saw in Session A that an organization can classify its costs in various ways, in particular in relation to:

- which costs are treated as direct costs and which as indirect;
- which costs are treated as what type of overhead.

This is important, since a standard costing system can identify a certain amount of overhead to each unit of production or service if the organization sees fit, as well as direct materials and labour.

Activity 16 ·   3 mins

Karl has also worked out that, for each hour he works on the rat cages, he incurs rent, rates, heating and insurance costs of £3. Remember he works for three and a half hours on each cage. By how much will the standard cost per cage rise if he takes overheads into account?

I hope you calculated that the standard cost will rise by £3.50 × 3 = £10.50 so the total standard cost will be £93.00.

Now let's see how differences between actual costs and standard costs (**variances**) can be calculated and analysed.

4 Variances from standard

Variances are the differences between what costs **actually are** and what they **should be** – the standard.

A variance can be either **adverse** (when the actual cost is higher than the standard) or **favourable** (when the cost is actually lower than the standard).

With a basic standard costing system, variances can be highlighted for:

- every material used;
- every type of direct labour;
- variable overheads (such as workshop heat and light).

Clearly, this detailed information is very important to managers who wish to control work. Notice that we are only looking here at the costs that fluctuate with levels of activity. These are the ones that are most likely to be controllable by first line managers.

The following diagram shows how an analysis of these work variances breaks down.

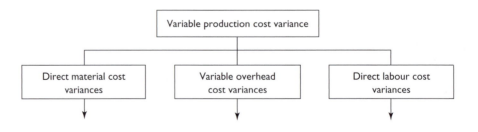

We shall use an analysis of materials and labour costs to illustrate that standard costing can help pinpoint variances and so improve control.

4.1 Direct material cost variances

Direct material cost variances can be divided into two types:

- usage variance;
- price variance.

Don't worry about the terminology too much. We have already seen the usage rate when we said that Karl uses 12 metres of timber. The price rate was £1.50 per metre.

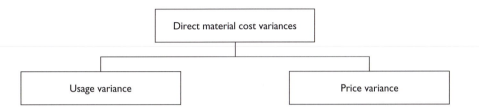

If an adverse usage variance occurs, it means that more material has been used than the standard indicated. This might have come about because inefficient methods meant that more scrap than expected was produced.

Activity 17 · 2 mins

A decision to improve a price variance by using cheaper materials can lead to more scrap and a worsening usage variance. The consequence of changes made in response to variances need careful consideration.

Who do you think is ultimately responsible for a usage variance?

_____

Who do you think is directly responsible for excessive scrap being produced?

_____

Ultimately, the production controller, or similarly named person, is responsible for a variance from standard usage. However, the first line manager is likely to have to account directly for scrap being higher than expected.

Now let's look at the direct labour cost variance.

4.2 Direct labour cost variances

Direct labour cost variances break down to:

- efficiency variance;
- idle time variance;
- rate variance.

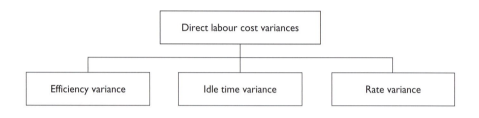

An adverse **efficiency** variance means that the work team spent longer making the product than the standard indicated. So, for instance, Karl spent 4 hours making a cage. Once again, we would need to know who was responsible and the reasons for the standard not being achieved.

An **idle time** variance is caused by the work team not having any work for a longer period than expected.

This could be caused, among other reasons, by:

- equipment breakdown;
- materials hold-up;
- a lack of power.

Activity 18

Suggest who or what you think would be responsible for each of these causes of an adverse idle time variance.

Equipment breakdown _____

Materials hold-up _____

Lack of power _____

EXTENSION 2
Calculating variances can be time-consuming. Computerization is used to provide us with variance information. This extension shows how a spreadsheet can be used to help with costing materials, labour and overheads in Sue Nugus' book *Financial Planning using Spreadsheets*.

In practice, things are often more complicated than they seem. There could be a number of contributory factors which different managers would have to account for. It's quite possible that you have suggested:

■ for equipment breakdown, the maintenance engineer;
■ for materials hold-up, the stock control department;
■ for lack of power, interruption of power supply owing to adverse weather conditions.

An adverse **rate** variance means that the work team costs for the time taken were more than was expected. This is most often because overtime has had to be paid, say because other work overran its time in a factory and so work had to be completed outside normal factory hours. Usually the production controller is responsible for this.

Another common cause of a labour rate variance is the use of more highly paid staff than was anticipated.

4.3 Calculating and presenting variances

Now that we have looked at the nature of variances and at some of their possible causes, we shall briefly calculate some simple variances and try to identify their significance.

Activity 19 · 10 mins

Despite Karl's careful preparation of a standard cost statement for the rat cages, he has now found that it has cost him £83.40 to produce one. He has used 12.5 metres of timber, which cost £20, and 7 square metres of wire mesh, which cost £15.40. He took four hours to make the cage. To try to save money, Karl paid himself only £48.00 for those four hours.

Fill in the variance statement below, in order to identify the causes of the total cost variance (the details have been filled in, and the calculation of the actual rate made, for the wire mesh).

Variance statement: Rat cage

	Quantity planned	Rate planned £	Standard cost (A) £	Quantity used	Actual rate £	Actual cost (B) £	Variance (A – B) £
Direct materials							
Wire mesh	6	2.00	12.00	7	2.20	15.40	3.40 (A)
Timber	12	1.50	18.00				
Direct labour							
Karl's time	3.5	15.00	52.50				
Standard cost			82.50		Actual cost		

You should have produced a statement like this.

Variance statement: Rat cage

	Quantity planned	Rate planned £	Standard cost (A) £	Quantity used	Actual rate £	Actual cost (B) £	Variance (A – B) £
Direct materials							
Wire mesh	6	2.00	12.00	7	2.20	15.40	3.40 (A)
Timber	12	1.50	18.00	12.5	1.60	20.00	2.00 (A)
Direct labour							
Karl's time	3.5	15.00	52.50	4	12.00	48.00	4.50 (F)
Standard cost			82.50		Actual cost	83.40	0.90 (A)

For each type of material, and for labour, we can break the variances down further to see exactly what the causes were (we know that there was no idle time).

Detailed variance statement: Rat cage

£

Wire mesh price variance	(7 metres × £0.20)	1.40 (A)	
Wire mesh usage variance	(1 × £2.00)	2.00 (A)	
Wire mesh variance (adverse)			£3.40 (A)
Timber price variance	(12.5 metres × £0.10)	1.25 (A)	
Timber usage variance	(0.5 metres × £1.50)	0.75 (A)	
Timber variance (adverse)			£2.00 (A)
Labour rate variance	(4 hours × £3.00)	12.00 (F)	
Labour efficiency variance	(0.5 hours × £15.00)	7.50 (A)	
Labour variance (favourable)			£4.50 (F)
Total cost variance			£0.90 (A)

Don't worry too much about how these detailed variances were calculated. What this statement shows us is what we intuitively knew already: Karl used more materials, and paid more for them per metre, than he expected, and also took longer than he expected to make the cage. By calculating these detailed variances, however, we have pinpointed and quantified the causes, and can then set about ways of reducing those variances that are unacceptable to Karl.

5 The value of standard costing

Standard costing, largely controlled by people, means that a lot of information about performance is gathered.

This leads us to two other advantages of standard costing:

- it's possible to achieve real economies through thinking in advance about the best materials to use, the best methods and so on;
- attention can be concentrated on the variances that **exceed** predetermined limits, rather than looking at all variances, some of which may be quite minor.

So an analysis of variances from standard costs can lead to a very detailed and far-reaching investigation of the problem. Perhaps you've already been involved in such investigations.

Identifying the responsible people is not a witch hunt; we are not looking for somebody to blame. The important step is to account for the variance so that better control can be established in future.

Self-assessment 2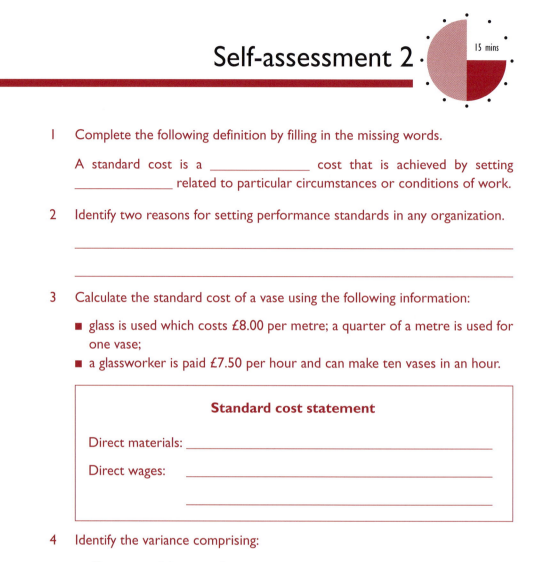

15 mins

1   Complete the following definition by filling in the missing words.

A standard cost is a _____ cost that is achieved by setting _____ related to particular circumstances or conditions of work.

2   Identify two reasons for setting performance standards in any organization.

_____

_____

3   Calculate the standard cost of a vase using the following information:

■ glass is used which costs £8.00 per metre; a quarter of a metre is used for one vase;

■ a glassworker is paid £7.50 per hour and can make ten vases in an hour.

Standard cost statement
Direct materials: _____
Direct wages: _____   _____

4   Identify the variance comprising:

■ direct material cost variances

_____

_____

■ direct labour cost variances

_____

_____

5   State what is indicated by favourable and adverse variances.

_____

_____

_____

_____

Answers to these questions can be found on pages 121–2.

6 Summary

- A standard cost is a cost calculated in advance and based on certain approved, specified work practices.

- Standard costing allows management to pinpoint variances precisely.

- Standard costs have two elements:

  - costs;
  - performance level.

- Standard performance levels should be based on expected standards and contain an allowable level of slack.

- Analysis of cost variances can lead to better cost control.

- The complete diagram of variances we have discussed is as shown below:

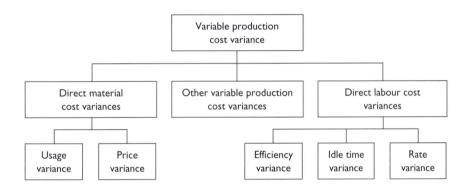

Session C
Controlling and reducing costs

1 Introduction

There are two main ways of controlling costs: effective monitoring (for which good information is needed) and active control. In this session we shall look first at how information can be collected and used, so that the person who controls costs is involved in monitoring them, and thus becomes highly cost-conscious.

Once costs have been collected (in cost units and cost centres), variances can be calculated. Most organizations accept that some level of variance is inevitable. However, at some point an adverse variance becomes unacceptable, and its adverse effects must be reduced. The first line manager may then be called upon to take more active control measures.

Sometimes a first line manager may be called on to reduce costs in a cost-cutting exercise. This is a more extreme form of cost control, which we shall also look at here.

Let's begin by looking at a few decisions in which cost information is very important.

2 Cost information and decisions

Consider the following Activity.

Activity 20

6 mins

Below are three questions on cost. For each one, jot down what you think would be the kind of decision that will be made as a result of the question being answered.

■ How many units of a proposed new product are likely to be sold, and what are the fixed costs? Once this question is answered, you would use the information to help you decide

_____

_____

■ How much does it cost to feed a patient in hospital for a week (a) using the hospital kitchen, (b) using an outside caterer? The answer to this question might lead the hospital authorities to investigate

_____

_____

_____

■ Can gas from a certain field be sold at more or less than the cost of extracting it? No further changes to working practices are possible. The answer to this question might lead to

_____

_____

_____

In the first instance, by knowing the fixed costs and a good estimation of likely sales, you can work out how the fixed costs can be spread over each unit sold. This will help in setting a price per unit to provide a profit. This is a pricing decision, based on break-even analysis.

In the second instance, hospital authorities can investigate whether it is cheaper to use their own kitchens and staff or to buy in the services of an outside caterer. There may well be things other than costs, such as the need to meet specific dietary needs or deal with rapidly changing volumes of patients, which affect the decision. This is a 'make or buy' decision.

Finally, gas fields in which the costs of extraction exceed the selling price are closed down because they are unprofitable. As with the earlier decisions, costs will not be the only things looked at, but they will be important. This is a closure decision.

The three kinds of decision we have looked at – pricing, 'make or buy' and closure – are major decisions made in a wide range of industries. Without collecting information about costs on a regular basis, organizations may not even know whether a particular process makes a profit or runs at a loss, or whether it would be cheaper for them to make something themselves or buy it in. Costs and cost information are therefore important to managers making a wide range of decisions.

2.1 Basic cost statements

A cost statement is often used to show the breakdown of costs so that the final cost of a product or service can be analysed.

Let's begin by looking at a manufacturing example. It's helpful in manufacturing to identify another cost: the **total factory cost**. This includes all the **prime** or direct costs plus all the indirect costs arising out of the need to keep the factory (but not the offices) running. Indirect costs are **factory overheads**.

Activity 21  10 mins

Write down one example of an appropriate cost beside each item shown in the following cost statement for the production of a car. I've given examples of factory overheads to help.

Cost statement of a car			
	£	£	Example of appropriate cost
Direct material		2,500	
Direct labour		2,500	
Prime cost		5,000	
Factory overheads		3,500	Production line, lighting, heating,
Total factory cost		8,500	health and safety expenditure
Administrative overheads	1,000		
Selling and distribution overheads (including dealer's profit margin)	1,500	2,500	
Total costs		11,000	
Profit		1,000	
Selling price		£12,000	

You could have thought of all sorts of things, since the manufacture, selling and distribution of a car is a complex process involving many people.

Under the prime cost heading, you could have identified any of the raw materials that go into a car and the wages of anybody directly involved in production.

Administration could be anything to do with purchasing, payments, stock control or any of the paperwork involved in running a business.

Selling and distribution would include advertising, promotions, delivering cars to the dealers and getting them in showroom condition.

Now let's see how this sort of analysis can be used if we adapt it slightly for an organization, such as a hospital, which provides a service.

We'll say it costs about £600 a week to keep a patient in a general ward in hospital.

Cost structure of patient care on general ward (cost per in-patient week)			
	£	£	Examples
Direct labour		250	Medical and nursing salaries
Direct materials		100	Drugs, medical supplies
Prime cost		350	
Administrative overheads	100		Clerical salaries, rates, telephone
General hospital overheads	150	250	Catering, cleaning costs and maintenance
Total costs		£600	

Once again, the costs are broken down into direct costs and overheads.

2.2 Cost units

Costs can be divided into direct costs and overheads. However, this analysis is only useful if the costs relate to an identifiable item, called a *cost unit*. In the example of the cost of producing a car, the car was the cost unit. In the case of the hospital, it was an in-patient week. Each organization defines its own cost units.

The most obvious cost unit is the finished product. For instance, a brewery may send out its beer in barrels or kegs which would be the cost units. A cement factory will probably send its cement out by the tonne, so will probably use a tonne of cement as a cost unit.

Cost units can be used by organizations that provide a service too.

Activity 22

4 mins

Jot down what you think might be the cost units used by:

■ swimming baths

_____

■ a school canteen

_____

■ letter delivery at Royal Mail

_____

Swimming baths would probably use a bather as a cost unit. A school canteen could use individual meals produced as a cost unit. Royal Mail is a more difficult problem. You could have suggested an individual letter or package for the sorting office, or an individual address for delivery staff.

In fact, a business can analyse any part of the workplace and work out appropriate cost units. For example, some of the cost units we might find in a car factory are:

■ final product – cost per car;
■ electricity cost – cost per kilowatt hour the production line is running;
■ computer running cost – cost per computer minute of operation;
■ canteen – cost per canteen meal.

In a complex organization, analysing costs at a more detailed level like this will help the people responsible for those costs to monitor them, and take action if necessary.

This leads us to the subject of cost centres.

3 Cost centres

A cost centre is a location where costs can be identified, grouped together and then finally related to a cost unit.

A cost centre is, in other words, a collection point for costs.

By a 'location' I mean something like:

- a department within a particular workplace;
- a work area;
- a machine or group of machines;
- a person, e.g. a hospital consultant.

The advantages of breaking down costs and collecting them in a number of cost centres are that:

- information on costs can be collected more easily;
- information on costs in different parts of the organization can be provided;
- managers of particular cost centres can be given standards against which costs can be controlled.

Identifying costs in cost centres helps to control costs in the various parts of the organization, and to control how each unit or department spends money.

The diagram below shows an example of three cost centres within an organization. Each cost centre collects:

- costs of materials and labour used within the centre;
- a proportion of the overheads for the whole organization.

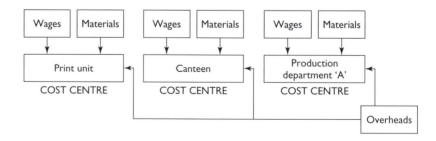

Collection of costs in cost centres

Activity 23

Look at the diagram on the previous page and decide into which cost centres you would collect the following costs:

Paper for digital print machine _____

Cook's wages _____

Wages of machine operator working in Department A _____

It looks as though paper for the digital print machine is a print unit cost; the cook's wages are a canteen cost; and the machine operator's wages are a cost incurred in production Department A. Each cost centre would collect the costs relevant to it.

The canteen and the print unit are providing a service to other parts of the organization. So we can distinguish between two types of cost centre:

- service centres, and
- product centres.

An important aim of a manufacturing organization is to make goods; that's how it earns its income. All services (such as the canteen, the stores, the maintenance department and so on) exist only to assist in that aim. Therefore, all costs must be finally transferred from the service centres to the product centres. The total costs of the product centre will then be spread over the cost units it produces.

For a building firm, the total cost of building houses is made up of many different individual costs. If the firm provides safety helmets for its workers, the cost of the helmets may be initially part of the materials costs for a 'safety department' cost centre. Ultimately these costs must appear in the cost of each house, the cost unit.

You may be thinking that this process sounds rather complicated and difficult to manage. It is, if it is not organized properly. Collecting costs is a detailed process that can only be done effectively by using cost codes for every item of cost. It is very often the role of the first line manager to ensure that the correct cost codes are created and used. So let's look at them now.

3.1 Cost codes

A good cost system enables costs to be:

- collected;
- analysed;
- controlled.

This means that we have to be able to find out precisely what expenses have been incurred in any part of the workplace, and we have to know how much we are spending in the workplace as a whole on different sorts of expense (overtime, electricity, stationery, etc.).

To help us do this a system of cost codes is often used. This will mean having two types of code:

- a special code for each cost centre, which will identify any costs incurred in that cost centre;
- a special code for each type of cost – such as stationery – wherever it occurs throughout the workplace.

By combining the cost centre code (for the accounts department, for example) and the code identifying the type of cost (stationery), we can identify how much has been spent on any particular item in any particular cost centre, and so control costs throughout the organization.

Let's look at how a cost coding system works.

Each workplace uses certain groups of numbers to mean particular things. These groups usually contain enough spare numbers for new kinds of cost to be added to the list of codes. For instance, a workplace with seven different cost centres may allocate the group of codes 01, 02, 03, . . . 18, 19 to cost centres, providing plenty of room to expand the list.

Let's look at a selection of likely cost codes for a general hospital.

Hospital cost centres	Codes	Items of expenditure	Codes
Ward 1	001	Ward sister's salary	025
Ward 2	002	Staff nurse's salary	026
Ward 3	003	Cleaner's wages	107
Theatre 1	098	Medical equipment	400–449
Theatre 2	099	Drugs	450–500
Pharmacy	171	Laundry assistant's wages	181
Physiotherapy department	264	Cleaning materials	600–630
Laundry	351	Cook's wages	197
Canteen	400		

Sister's salary on Ward 2 will be coded 002 025. Cleaning materials for Ward 3 could be coded 003 610 or 003 622 or 003 630, because the range indicates different codes for different types of cleaning material.

Activity 24 · 5 mins

Cost codes must be clear and well understood for them to be effective. A code for 'sundry expenses' is often overused.

Work out codes for the following. Where you have a range of numbers, choose any one from within that range.

■ Theatre 1 staff nurse's salary _____ _____

■ Theatre 2 medical equipment _____ _____

■ Physiotherapy department medical equipment _____ _____

■ Drug coded 459 and ordered for the pharmacy _____ _____

■ Canteen cook's wages _____ _____

The answer to this Activity can be found on page 124.

Activity 25 · 2 mins

Here is a list of some costs in the hospital to which cost codes have been allocated. One of them seems rather suspicious and would need to be checked out. (Tick the suspect code.)

098 107 ☐

001 026 ☐

400 457 ☐

According to these cost codes, the canteen has been ordering drugs (400 457)! This sounds very worrying and needs investigating urgently.

What this activity shows us is that information on costs is not only used to help us minimize costs – it also helps to make sure that costs are only occurring where they should be.

A system of cost codes means that everybody in the workplace describes each kind of cost in the same way. Information about costs is simplified and is presented in a standard way, making it easier to interpret and analyse.

Cost codes, made up of cost centre code and type of cost code, also mean that every single cost can be traced to a certain cost centre, improving control.

Identifying certain kinds of expense by the same code throughout the workplace means that you can also see how much you are spending on certain things (overtime or electricity, for instance), overall. This will help in deciding how best to utilize resources, to minimize expenditure or to reduce total costs.

4 Control through cost centres

Whether the cost centre is a work area, a machine or a group of machines or a team of people, it could well be you, as first line manager, who is responsible for maintaining the cost centre and controlling the associated costs.

You might have to:

- requisition materials (materials);
- authorize and collect time sheets (labour);
- control the level of overhead costs in your work area, such as electricity or telephone use.

Let's look at how materials and wages costs are collected in appropriate cost centres.

The collection and application of overhead costs is rather more complex, but we'll look at that later.

4.1 Cost centres and materials costs

A first line manager may have the responsibility for:

- raising a materials requisition for goods in the workplace stores which are needed for the job;
- raising a purchase requisition for goods needed for the job, which are not in the stores and so have to be specially bought;
- taking care of materials once they are in the work area.

The diagram below shows an outline of the movement of paperwork and goods which take place when items are requested. The sharp-edged boxes denote paperwork, and the round-edged boxes denote locations.

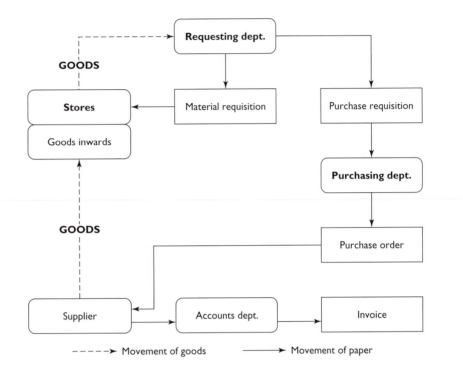

Movement of paperwork and goods

Activity 26 · 10 mins

Look at Figure 2 and identify three people or departments, apart from the requesting department and the supplier, who have a part to play in the materials costing system.

Against each one write down briefly what you think their responsibilities are.

_____

_____

_____

_____

_____

Here is my breakdown of the roles played by various departments in the materials costing system.

- Purchasing department/purchasing officer:

  - ordering goods;
  - keeping lists of approved suppliers;
  - checking supplier's prices.

- Goods inward department:

  - receiving goods;
  - checking quality and quantity of goods supplied;
  - issuing goods-received notes to accounts department.

- Stores department:

  - storage and care of goods in store;
  - keeping records of receipts and issues to and from stores and current balances of items held;
  - issuing purchase requisitions when stock levels fall;
  - issuing supplies for certain jobs on receipt of a proper materials requisition note.

- Accounting department:

  - receiving and checking invoices against orders and goods received notes;
  - keeping accounting records for the entire workplace;
  - paying the supplier;
  - costing materials for particular jobs;
  - recording cost information.

Activity 27

Look back at Session B on standard costing. How do you think a standard cost statement for making a particular item or providing a particular service would help a first line manager in requesting materials and controlling their cost?

_____

_____

_____

I hope you can see that a standard cost statement helps the practical process in at least two ways. First, the manager can see what items are needed for a product or service, such as wire mesh and timber for a rat cage. Secondly, the manager can see how much they are expecting to pay for that material.

Without this sort of information, the materials requisition might just as well say: 'enough stuff to make a rat cage, and hang the expense!'

4.2 Cost centres and labour costs

You are likely to be directly involved in the control and recording of labour costs. Your position gives you a degree of authority over your work team and responsibility for:

- controlling timekeeping, particularly important if you are monitoring a flexi-time system;
- controlling quality of performance;
- recording time spent on individual jobs, if applicable;
- passing time records to the appropriate department for analysis.

Other departments which will be involved to some extent in the labour costing system are:

- wages department;
- accounts department;
- personnel department.

Time sheets or similar forms to record time spent at work are used to help in the calculation of labour costs.

Time Sheet

Name *A Brown*
Department (cost centre) *Assembly shop*

Employee no. *740*
Grade: *M*
Week ending *25/6*

| Date | AM | | PM | | Excess hours | | Total hours |
	In	Out	In	Out	In	Out	
21/6	*7.58*	*12.01*	*1.00*	*5.01*			*8.00*
22/6	*7.55*	*12.00*	*1.00*	*5.05*			*8.00*
23/6	*8.00*	*12.00*	*1.00*	*5.00*	*6.00*	*9.00*	*11.00*
24/6	*7.55*	*12.00*	*1.00*	*4.55*			*8.00*
25/6	*7.59*	*12.01*	*1.02*	*5.00*			*8.00*

The time sheet, illustrated above, has to be analysed before being passed to the wages department.

Activity 28 · 5 mins

Using the information on the time sheet, fill in the blank spaces below, assuming a normal working week of 40 hours.

Regular time _____ hours at £6.00   £ _____

Over time _____ hours at £9.00   £ _____

Gross earnings   £ _____

The answer to this Activity can be found on page 124.

The first line manager is usually directly responsible for confirming that the records of how much time the work team has spent are true. In a flexi-time system, appropriate core time must be confirmed (i.e. employees should be at work when required) as well as attending for the appropriate total time within the flexible working pattern. But the team leader's responsibilities for labour cost control don't end here.

Typical additional responsibilities would include:

■ allocating time to individual jobs;
■ allocating an appropriate grade of staff to a particular job;
■ controlling the amount of time spent on individual jobs by each member of the work team;
■ keeping idle time, such as travel time, to a minimum.

I hope you can see that knowing how much time should be spent by what kinds of staff, and how much that time should cost, will be useful to the manager in performing these tasks. As with materials, this information will come from the standard cost card.

To the practical responsibilities we can add the 'paperwork responsibilities' which go with the job:

Cost control is only worthwhile if it saves more for an organization than the costs of its operation. Too much time or paperwork and you should question its relevance.

■ confirming that cost details shown for each job are correct;
■ passing costs per job to the accounts department for analysis;
■ verifying idle time costs;
■ passing details of idle time costs to the accounts department so that it can be properly accounted for. (Generally it needs to be apportioned on some reasonable basis over all jobs.)

A computer report which analyses time and services provided, is normally the key document in transferring labour cost information from a particular work area to whoever is responsible for summarizing cost information.

Activity 29

5 mins

A Brown, whose time sheet we saw in Activity 28, spent the whole of Monday, Tuesday and Wednesday starting and completing the assembly of Product X.

Fill in the actual labour cost for Product X on the computer report below. What does the comparison against the expected cost tell you?

PRODUCT X

Assembly costs

	Actual cost	Expected cost	
Grade of labour used:	M	N	
Regular time:	___ hours at £ ___	22 hours at £7.50	165.00
Overtime:	___ hours at £ ___	0	0.00
	___		
Total assembly labour:			£165.00

The comparison against expected cost tells me

You should have come up with the following calculation.

PRODUCT X

Assembly costs

	Actual cost			Expected cost	
Grade of labour used:	M			N	
Regular time:	24 hours at £6.00	144.00		22 hours at £7.50	165.00
Overtime:	3 hours at £9.00	27.00		0	0.00
Total assembly labour:		£171.00			£165.00

I hope you can see that the cost has exceeded what was expected. This was because a lower grade of employee was used, who spent more time than was expected, including overtime.

How could the first line manager have controlled this overrun of costs? It depends on the circumstances. Perhaps a grade N employee was not available, or was sick. If so, the manager needs to consider reworking the work schedules so that the right numbers of the right grades of staff are always available. Perhaps training could be implemented to upgrade the grade M staff.

Alternatively, the situation may have been outside the manager's control. Product X might have been planned to arrive when grade N staff were available, but have been delayed by another department.

Now that we have raised the issue of control, let's have a look for a moment at the question of idle time.

Common causes are:

- equipment breakdown;
- power failure;
- waiting for work to be scheduled;
- waiting for materials or tools;
- waiting for instructions.

Idle time is not normally charged directly against the job, but is regarded as a production overhead, or overhead incurred in providing a service. But if the fault can be traced to one particular department, it may be charged against that department.

For instance, say a factory maintenance programme, scheduled to be completed over a weekend shutdown runs late and production time is lost once everybody is back at work.

It seems obvious that in this case the fault can be traced back to the maintenance department and the cost of the idle time will be charged to it. In that case all the managers in the maintenance department have got some explaining to do.

4.3 Cost centres and overheads

Some overheads belong entirely to one cost centre, while some can be shared among several cost centres.

Where an overhead can belong entirely to one cost centre we say that it is **allocated** to the appropriate cost centre. The first line manager of that cost centre will bear the responsibility for controlling these overhead costs within the cost centre.

Activity 30 · 3 mins

Think of two overhead costs from your own workplace which could be allocated entirely to one cost centre.

_____

_____

It's unlikely that we've thought of the same things, but here are a couple of examples that spring to mind:

■ the wages of a manager in the food hall of a large superstore will be allocated to the food hall cost centre;
■ the cost of an advertising promotion will be allocated to the marketing cost centre.

Activity 31

3 mins

Here are some more overhead costs, which are similar in that they can be allocated entirely to individual cost centres. Against each one, write down which of the following three classes of overheads it belongs to: production overheads, administration overheads or selling and distribution overheads.

■ Wages of managers working entirely within a particular production department.

_____

■ Paint, oil and grease used in a certain production department.

_____

■ Wages of receptionists.

_____

■ Travelling expenses of sales staff.

_____

The first two costs are production overheads, the wages of receptionists are likely to be an administrative overhead and the travelling expenses of the sales staff are a selling overhead. Each of these could be allocated directly and entirely to one cost centre, and the responsibility of controlling them is that of the cost centre manager.

Often, though, overhead costs have to be spread over a number of cost centres. These costs are controlled first of all in one cost centre and then **apportioned** between other cost centres, using an agreed method of deciding how they should be shared out or apportioned.

Here are some overhead costs that might be apportioned among various departments. I've also shown the cost centre where the cost would initially be controlled, and suggested a possible method for apportioning the cost between all departments.

Type of cost	Cost centre where cost is initially controlled	Possible method of apportionment
Rent and rates	Property manager	Floor area occupied by various departments
Lighting and heating	Plant engineer	Building volume occupied by various departments
Insurance of equipment	Administration manager	Value of equipment in various departments

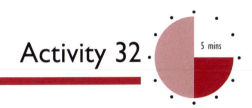

Activity 32

5 mins

In the space provided below, write down which cost centre you think should initially control each overhead and suggest a method by which they could fairly be apportioned.

Type of cost	Cost centre where cost is initially controlled	Possible method of apportionment
Staff welfare		
Advertising for staff		
Building repairs		

Here are my suggestions. You may have thought of other equally reasonable suggestions, so don't feel that our answers have to be the same.

Where possible it is preferable to **allocate** overheads directly to cost centres, if there are clear and agreed bases for doing so rather than to **apportion** them between cost centres, as the overheads are identified as being generated by, or the responsibility of, those cost centres.

Type of cost	Cost centre where cost is initially controlled	Possible method of apportionment
Staff welfare	Personnel manager	Number of staff per department
Advertising for staff	Personnel manager	Number of vacancies notified per department
Building repairs	Building and works manager	Floor area per department

There is no hard-and-fast method of apportioning overheads. But methods should be logical.

How much control can first line managers have over costs that have been apportioned to them, rather than allocated to them directly?

The answer is somewhere between very little and none.

Looking at the example above, you should be able to see that the first line manager of a department cannot control at all how much the personnel manager spends on staff welfare. Whether they are charged at all for advertising staff vacancies can be controlled to some extent by limiting the number of staff being recruited. But how much per vacancy the personnel department spends is beyond their control.

Activity 33 · 2 mins

How far can a departmental first line manager control the costs apportioned to the department for building repairs?

_____

_____

_____

How much money the Building and Works Manager spends is beyond the first line manager's control, as is (in the short term) the chargeable floor area occupied by the department. The only way the first line manager can exercise some control is in trying to ensure that the department doesn't cause building repairs to be necessary.

It is not necessary for you to know more about the accounting process of allocating, approving or transferring costs. It is this awareness of costs, not accounting manipulations, which is the key to success. Cost consciousness is important managerial behaviour. Apart from being aware of information on costs how is a cost-conscious attitude fostered?

5 Cost consciousness

We've seen that controlling and keeping down costs demands continued effort. You have to be permanently on the look-out for performance levels falling, materials and equipment being wrongly used, bottlenecks, idle time, untidy and slipshod ways of working and so on.

Clearly you can only do so much yourself. You need the support of the work team in looking for and maintaining ways of keeping down costs, and in keeping records of what is actually happening in your work areas.

If one person tries to keep costs down on their own by turning off lights when they go out, it will have little effect. But if that person can persuade a dozen others to do the same, increasing amounts can be saved.

So what can we do to make the work team aware of the costs and become enthusiastic about keeping them down?

Activity 34 · 4 mins

S/NVQ D6

This Activity may provide the basis of evidence for your S/NVQ portfolio. If you are intending to take this course of action, it might be better to write your answers on separate sheets of paper.

Suggest two ways in which you think you could make your work team more cost conscious. How would you implement your suggestions?

_____

_____

_____

_____

Typical answers might include:

- getting the work team more involved;
- encouraging them to make suggestions;
- offering prizes for suggestions on how to keep costs down;
- passing on information about costs;
- telling them when costs increase or decrease.

Perhaps you might talk to your work team or put up notices and then follow up with meetings, discussions and so on.

If you are compiling an S/NVQ portfolio you may be able to use notices and testimony from your work team members and your manager as the basis of possible acceptable evidence.

5.1 Spotting the need for cost consciousness and control

To be really successful at being conscious of costs and hence controlling them, you have to be aware of those areas of your work team's operations where costs may be a problem. One way to do this is by analysing costs in terms of variances. As we have seen, these show both the cause of the cost and its size. Together the analysis allows us to both spot a problem and do something about it.

Activity 35

5 mins

Look at the possible adverse variances below. Against each one, jot down what you could do to affect them.

Materials

Adverse price variance

_____

Adverse usage variance

_____

Labour

Adverse efficiency variance

_____

Adverse rate variance

_____

Adverse idle time variance

Overheads

Adverse price variance

You will probably have jotted down answers based on what is familiar to you, but in general I expect our answers will not be very different from each other.

Materials price variance	Check that the best price possible is being obtained for materials from suppliers
Materials usage variance	Check that there is not excessive wastage in the process
Labour efficiency variance	Check that staff are working effectively and have all the equipment and training that they need to do so
Labour rate variance	Check that staff of the right grade are being used on appropriate work, and that unnecessary overtime is not being worked
Labour idle time variance	Check that work is flowing smoothly into the work team, and that there are no hold-ups such as for machine breakdowns
Overhead variance	Check that the work team is not incurring unnecessary overheads and that prices obtained are reasonable.

One other factor to bear in mind: it is always possible that the standard against which variances are measured has become out of date. This means that it is not your control of costs that is in question, but the relevance of the variances in the first place.

The three keys to success in raising cost consciousness are:

- **involvement;**
- **communication;**
- **feedback.**

5.2 Involvement and communication

Cost consciousness means treating costs in the workplace as though *your* money was going to be used to pay for them. Successfully finding ways of keeping costs down means keeping an eye on your spending all the time, rather than looking for one good idea. In the end your job and the money you earn depend on a successful operation, of which controlling costs is an important element.

We need to communicate with people about cost if we want them to become involved. The trouble is, much of the information used in the workplace to monitor costs is likely to be in the form of financial statements that are not easy to understand and which can easily put people off.

You and other team leaders need to give your team members information about costs in terms that are relevant, timely and in an appropriate place.

Activity 36 · 3 mins

Here are two ways of communicating information about a quarterly electricity bill.

Tick whichever you think would make you more conscious of the cost of the electricity you are using.

a ☐

> NOTICE
>
> The electricity bill for the last quarter was:
>
> £2,321.41
>
> *Save it!*

b ☐

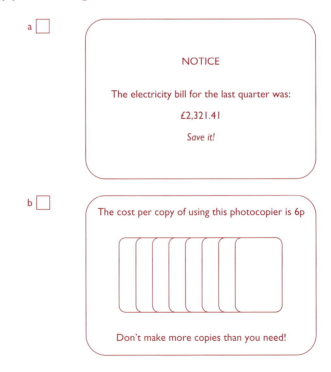

> The cost per copy of using this photocopier is 6p
>
> Don't make more copies than you need!

We can make a case for saying that either of these would be effective for different people. Let's look at (a) first.

Sometimes the sheer size of a sum of money, like the cost of this electricity bill, can give people a jolt. £2,321.41 sounds a lot more serious than 6p per photocopied sheet.

However, large figures quickly baffle us and tend not to mean a lot. Electricity bills of £1,500, £2,400 or £13,967 all sound equally terrifying if our quarterly bill at home is about £100.

It's all too easy to feel that such a large sum is nothing to do with us. We feel that we didn't contribute much to the bill in the first place and there is nothing we can do to reduce it.

Knowing that each photocopy we take costs 6p is likely to make a bigger impression, because it relates directly to what we are doing, particularly if we have to use a counter that charges copies directly to our budget.

So, I would say that (b) is more likely to raise peoples awareness of the costs and prompt them to try to do something about them than (a).

This sort of information doesn't just have to be in the form of some kind of notice. Just saying something like:

> 'This aluminium wrapper is £50 a roll now. I don't think we should let it get knocked about.'

or

> 'We've just spent £200 having these blades reset. Better make sure that no grit gets in there.'

may have a similar effect.

Activity 37   2 mins

Refer back to the two notices about costs.

Which do you think is a more effective place to display the information these notices contain: on the canteen notice-board or above the photocopier?

Information about costs will make more impact if it is provided where the cost is about to be incurred and just as it's going to be incurred.

What we read as we are about to use a piece of equipment is harder to avoid than information on the canteen notice-board.

Of course, like many notices, we can get used to them in time and fail to see them. It is useful to replace them with new and different, but striking, notices regularly.

We can say that information about costs needs to be:

- in a form we can relate to;
- at the time and place the cost is incurred.

5.3 Feedback

Now let's look at feedback – the response you give to the work team's efforts to keep costs down or to their suggestions for cost savings.

Activity 38

3 mins

Suppose somebody in your workplace suggests a change to a certain process that will reduce costs. The change is approved and made, and there is an article about it in the house newspaper. Write down two important pieces of information that you would hope to find in the article.

_____

_____

You may have had several ideas but I hope among them would be:

- the name of the person who made the suggestion;
- how much money it will save.

If we are to be aware of costs, we want to know how much we're saving by our efforts. Certainly, if we're going to maintain an interest in costs, we need to know that we're making progress. By recognizing who suggested the cost saving, further emphasis is placed on its importance.

Of course, not all suggestions are necessarily good ideas.

Activity 39

2 mins

Somebody in your work team suggests changing your computer stationery supplier. He has spoken to a representative from an alternative supplier and obtained some prices. On the face of it, it looks as though the alternative supplier's prices are less than you are currently paying. Investigating further, you find that the prices apply only to larger volume purchases than you would make and that the existing supplier has a better reputation for quality and reliability.

Tick the appropriate box to indicate if you would:

a let the subject drop because telling your work team member might discourage him from making further suggestions ☐

b tell him that it wasn't a workable idea ☐

c thank him for taking the trouble to find out about the alternative supplier and explain who you weren't going to take up the suggestion ☐

You probably chose (c).

EXTENSION 3
Chapter 7 of David Doyle's book *Cost Control: A Strategic Guide* looks at cost responsibility and awareness in some depth.

It is easy to understand that, even though the suggestion isn't taken up, people need feedback on their ideas if they are to maintain an interest. However, it's not easy to remember to supply that feedback when we're under a lot of pressure to do all sorts of other jobs.

It's worth making the effort, however. If you don't encourage cost consciousness, even when it is not directly useful, it won't be there when you need it.

6 Checklists for controlling costs

Finding ways of controlling costs and keeping them down depends upon thinking about every situation in the workplace and asking whether we are making the best possible use of the resources involved and doing the task in question in the most efficient way.

The questions we need to ask ourselves, and the answers we will get, will vary with the job and the workplace.

I hope you will find the following checklists help you to channel your thoughts as you examine your work area to ensure you have your workteam operating efficiently. Use the space provided to make your own notes.

6.1 Checklist for the work team

- Do I use people with the right amount of skill for the job in hand?

  _____

- Do I use highly paid people for low level work? If so, why? Can it be avoided?

  _____

  _____

- Are salaries reviewed regularly?

  _____

- Is all our overtime necessary?

  _____

- What causes idle time?

  - Lack of materials? ☐ _____

  - Lack of available equipment? ☐ _____

  - Lack of precise instructions? ☐ _____

  - Lack of supervision? ☐ _____

- Is the work team good about timekeeping?

  _____

- Are all the members of the work team fully trained?

  _____

- Is the work team fully competent?

  _____

- Do their skills need bringing up to date?

■ Is career development taken seriously?

_____

■ Are they willing to try new ideas?

_____

■ Is there any information they would like to know about the workplace, the organization or the product?

_____

■ How often do I make a point of chatting to them about themselves and the job?

_____

■ Do I ever have to explain what I want done several times?

_____

■ Should I write instructions for any tasks the work team do?

_____

■ Are written instructions up to date, in the right place and readable?

_____

■ Do I give the work team feedback on their performance regularly (not just when things go wrong)?

_____

■ What is our absenteeism record like?

_____

■ How many of the work team have left in the past two years? Why?

_____

■ Have the work team any special skills or knowledge which we're not using?

_____

■ What records do I keep to help make the best possible use of the work team?

_____

6.2 Checklist for materials

- Do we use the cheapest materials for the purpose without reducing the quality?

  _____

- Do we run out of materials? Why?

  _____

- Do we have any out-of-date materials? Why?

  _____

- Are any materials damaged during storage?

  _____

- What control have I over:

  - production materials?

  - consumables – bags, stationery, paper, oil, grease, packing materials, cleaning materials, etc.?

  _____

  _____

- Is scrap or waste material increasing/decreasing? Is work having to be done again to reach appropriate standards? Why?

  _____

- Is the workplace clean and tidy? How often do I check housekeeping?

  _____

6.3 Checklist for overheads

- Do I report equipment faults as soon as they occur?

  _____

- Do I keep a record of the date and reason for machine failure?

  _____

- Is all our equipment regularly maintained?

  _____

- How fully used is the equipment for which I am responsible?

  _____

- Could we get rid of any out-of-date machines?

  _____

- Can I improve the layout of the equipment in my work area?

  _____

- Are any machines standing idle? Why?

  _____

- Do we switch off lights and power when they are not needed?

  _____

- Do we backup overnight whenever possible? Do we reroute calls through a cheaper call provider, or use email?

  _____

- What changes would I like to introduce in the way we work which will make us more efficient?

  _____

- Which departments do I need to help me to do this?

  _____

  _____

  _____

7 Cost reduction

So far we have looked at controlling costs within a situation where the same level of operations is being carried out. But there are times when an organization has to make difficult decisions about what it is doing, how and where.

A business may be losing money, or a non-profit organization may have lost funding. There may be no choice but to 'cut costs' by:

■ closing down parts of its operations;
■ ceasing to make an unprofitable product or to provide a service that is not cost-effective;
■ outsourcing a service that is currently provided in-house, so that it is provided more economically by someone outside the organization.

Although these decisions will be made by senior managers, as a first line manager you may become caught up in this cost reduction process.

More than ever, it is important in this case to:

■ have information (on what costs need reducing and how and when this will be done);
■ communicate with your work team (to provide information and feedback and to involve them).

In some ways cost reduction can be said to be a more extreme form of cost control; but as it usually involves a cutback in the scale of operations it is a more difficult and painful process, often leading to redundancies, and the sale of buildings and machinery.

Activity 40

The School Meals Service has informed all school meals managers that their individual meals service must break even or be closed down and replaced by private contractors.

Isabel Smith, a school meals manager, can produce and sell a maximum of 1,000 meals per week.

She is told her weekly fixed overheads are £2,000. Education authority policy is to charge £1.50 per meal and Isabel cannot alter this.

She calculates that the variable costs per meal, all raw materials, are £0.50.

Work out the break-even for Isabel's canteen.

$$\frac{\text{Fixed overheads}}{\text{Contribution}} = \underline{\hspace{2cm}} = \underline{\hspace{2cm}} \text{ meals}$$

We can see that Isabel's position is fairly desperate! Here are her break-even calculations.

$$\frac{£2,000}{£1.00} = 2,000 \text{ meals.}$$

She cannot produce 2,000 meals because her limit for production and sales is 1,000. Unless she is allowed to increase prices drastically, close-down seems inevitable.

If she could raise her prices to £2.50, her surplus would be £2.00 per meal and, if she could sell her maximum number of meals (1,000), she would just break even.

Activity 41

S/NVQ
D6

This Activity may provide the basis of appropriate evidence for your S/NVQ portfolio. If you are intending to take this course of action, it might be better to write your answers on separate sheets of paper.

Have you been faced with such a problem as described above, requiring you to control your resources or make recommendations for the use of your resources so that costs can be cut?

Write down the tasks you had to complete and the reasons you were given for the changes needed.

_____

_____

_____

_____

_____

_____

Your response will be related to your own job. Perhaps you had to contribute to a decision whether a member of your work team should be made redundant or to think about whether a new piece of equipment would prove cheaper than one or two new people in the long term.

Self-assessment 3

1 a Name the two types of cost included in prime cost.

_____

_____

   b What additional costs are added to prime cost to arrive at the total factory cost?

_____

2 State what is meant by a cost centre.

_____

3 Identify the three characteristics of a good cost system.

_____

_____

_____

4 State the three keys to success in making a work team more cost conscious.

_____

_____

_____

5 How would you ensure that a worker's attention was drawn to information about costs?

_____

_____

_____

6 Why is it useful to use a checklist when examining your work area for ways to decrease costs?

_____

_____

_____

Answers to these questions can be found on page 122.

8 Summary

- Managers need cost information to make decisions.

- Direct costs are related to the individual unit produced, e.g. cost of raw materials.

- Overhead costs cannot be directly attributed to any one unit of production or service provided.

- Cost units are identifiable items against which the costs of a company, department or other defined part of the organization can be related.

- Cost centres are locations where costs can be conveniently collected and grouped.

- A cost coding system can be used for tracking every cost in the workplace.

- Direct material and labour costs are collected in cost centres and charged directly to the job. Overheads are also applied to job costs; many are estimates.

- To make the work team cost conscious:

  - involve them;
  - pass on information;
  - given them feedback.

- Information about costs needs to be:

  - in simple terms which we can relate to;
  - available where and when the costs are incurred.

Session D
What is a budget?

 ## 1 Introduction

How would you feel if you were never sure if you would be paid on pay-day or not?

To ensure that you do get paid on the right day, your organization needs to plan and to control the ways in which it spends and receives money so that enough cash is available to pay wages and salaries when due. The organization draws up a plan indicating how it expects money to flow in and out. This plan is better known as a budget.

You probably do the same at home, planning how to use your income. You budget, your employer prepares a budget and, of course, the country as a whole budgets.

Each year, the Chancellor of the Exchequer presents a Budget to Parliament. Its aim is to achieve things which are part of the government's policy on how best to run the country.

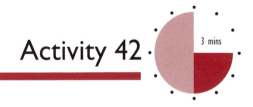

Activity 42

3 mins

Write down three things the Chancellor might try to achieve through the annual Budget.

_____

_____

_____

Typical examples might be to:

- improve public services;
- reduce inflation;
- combat unemployment;
- help small businesses;
- win the next election!

Whatever plans and policies the government has, they all have to be financed. The Budget is all about getting hold of and using money.

To achieve this, the Chancellor might introduce policies to:

- cut or tighten control over major items of expenditure;
- switch expenditure and resources from one item to another;
- use a variety of financial incentives and penalties.

The national Budget requires a lot of analysis, planning negotiations and juggling with resources. It covers both national income and national expenditure. All budgets work in similar ways; just the amounts involved differ.

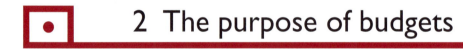

2 The purpose of budgets

Think about your own workplace for a moment. Your work team may be earning income through the sales it achieves or the services it supplies.

Or it might be contributing to profit (the surplus of income over costs) in one or two other ways.

directly, by purchasing, manufacturing or processing materials, to produce goods that are sold	**indirectly**, by such things as designing, controlling, maintaining equipment, or providing services to customers or other work teams

Whatever it does, your work team is certain to incur expenditure (costs), in doing its job. Almost certainly, the organization you belong to will have prepared a budget for its expenditure. If it generates income directly, then there will be a budget for that as well.

A budget can be described as:

a quantitative plan of action prepared in advance of a defined period of time.

Let's look at this definition more closely.

■ **A budget is quantitative.**

That means it must be stated in figures; in practice this usually means in sums of money. A general statement of what you intend to do may be useful, but it's not a budget.

■ **A budget is prepared in advance.**

A budget must be drawn up *before* the period to which it refers. Figures produced during or after the period may be important, but they are not part of a budget.

■ **A budget relates to a particular period.**

Budgets are drawn up for a certain specific period (often, though not always, one year). An open-ended financial plan for the future isn't a budget.

■ **A budget is a plan of action.**

This is perhaps the most important point of all. A budget can't be a definite statement of fact, because it relates to something which hasn't happened yet. It is what the organization is planning will happen.

Conditions may change during the budget period, which means the budget will be inaccurate. Like all plans, budgets seldom turn out to be totally correct predictions of the future. Even so, they can still be useful in guiding the actions of those using them. This guidance role is very important.

Of course, you must know what you are trying to achieve before planning. Everything else depends on that.

'Knowing what to achieve' is referred to in business as an **objective**.

The objectives of your workplace will depend to some extent on what kind of organization it is and may be short, medium or long term. Manufacturing industries, for example, have to make a profit. Local government services have to provide a certain level of service. A nationalized industry may be required to achieve a planned return on capital invested.

Some other examples of objectives are:

■ to make a profit of 30% on a certain product;
■ to increase the share of the market by 5% for a certain product;

- to improve service to the public in certain areas;
- to survive commercially for a financial year (this is particularly relevant to new, small businesses).

To achieve any of these objectives needs planning and will probably involve the production of budgets.

Activity 43

3 mins

Write down **two** different kinds of budget that are used in your organization to meet its objectives. One example would be a sales budget.

_____

_____

The budgets listed below are all common types. Perhaps your suggestions are among them, though you could well have thought of others too.

- Sales budget.
- Production budget.
- Research and development budget.
- Training budget.
- Departmental costs budget.
- Cash budget.

All budgets are important, although it is arguable that the cash budget is most important because without cash a business cannot survive.

Let's look briefly at sales budgets and cash budgets, to make sure we understand what they mean.

In a **sales budget**, a forecast is made of the sales the business will make during the relevant period. This may be broken down by section or department. Knowing how much you plan to sell is essential, in order to decide how much raw materials you will buy, how many employees you will need, and so on.

In a **cash budget** the business will forecast:

- what cash will be received and paid out during the budget period;
- the timing of receipts and payments;
- the bank balance or overdraft for each month.

The cash budget is especially important for small, newly established businesses.

Activity 44

2 mins

Who do you think would need to see the cash budget of a newly established business? Write down **one** suggestion.

_____

_____

EXTENSION 4
Assignment 14 in *The Business Plan Workbook*, by C. Barrow, P. Barrow and R. Brown, gives illustrations of the situations faced by businesses that have and have not prepared a cash budget.

You may have thought of a number of possibilities. The one I had in mind was the bank manager who will want to examine the cash forecasts of a new business, and will almost certainly insist on a cash budget before authorizing a loan for a new business.

However, I don't want to give the impression that it is only new, small businesses which find cash budgets important. Organizations, large and small, use them, and so do charities and social clubs. Everyone needs cash.

3 Beginning a budget

Here, we are going to think about the beginning of the budget process. We'll start with manufacturing industry – in a business which makes and sells something.

We need first to identify the critical factor which influences all the budgets in a certain workplace. The factor influences all other budgets, and is called the **key** or **limiting budget factor**.

In practice:

- the **sales budget** is the commonest limiting budget factor in established commercial businesses;
- the **cash budget** is the commonest limiting budget factor in newly established small businesses.

Sometimes the **production budget** is the limiting budget factor, although this is less common.

In a non-profit organization, the limiting budget factor is likely to be the availability of funds.

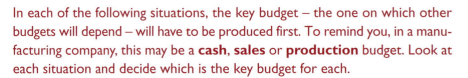

Activity 45 · 4 mins

In each of the following situations, the key budget – the one on which other budgets will depend – will have to be produced first. To remind you, in a manufacturing company, this may be a **cash**, **sales** or **production** budget. Look at each situation and decide which is the key budget for each.

	Key Budget	
Firm A exists in a highly competitive market and currently sells 500 units per month. It plans to increase this to 600 units per month in the coming year and, in fact, has the capacity to produce 750 units per month.	Cash	☐
	Sales	☐
	Production	☐
Firm B is the sole supplier of a specialist component. It can sell all it produces and more.	Cash	☐
	Sales	☐
	Production	☐
Firm C is a small business with a large overdraft. It is currently owed a great deal of money, and its bank insists that the overdraft cannot be extended.	Cash	☐
	Sales	☐
	Production	☐
Firm D is a haulage contractor with a fleet of ten lorries on the road that has been offered a contract to transport 12 lorry-loads of goods to Southern Europe on a weekly basis. The firm cannot afford to purchase additional lorries.	Cash	☐
	Sales	☐
	Production	☐

Here is what I would say is the key budget, on which all other budgets would depend, for each of these firms.

- For Firm A, it's a sales budget. The firm must sell more. Everything else, including production, will follow from that.
- For Firm B, it's a production budget. The firm has to produce more. If it achieves this then extra sales will follow.
- For Firm C, it's a cash budget. The most important thing is for the firm to earn cash at the moment. This might even mean that the firm would have to refuse a potentially profitable contract if it didn't bring in cash quickly enough.
- For Firm D, the key is the cash budget because the firm does not have enough cash to buy more lorries to provide the transport service offered.

4 Why do we need budgets?

Some people think of a budget as something that restricts what we want or need to do. It certainly can be very frustrating when the constraints of a budget, drawn up by accountants who (you may feel) have no understanding of your problems, prevent you from taking certain actions in your job.

See if you recognize any of the following situations or something similar.

The training budget of a hospital has been spent. A nursing sister is refused permission to go on a course to learn how to use a new piece of equipment for monitoring heart disease. She is concerned because she feels that patient care may suffer.

The entertainments budget of a growing electronics firm is exhausted. The sales manager is unable to offer the kind of hospitality he would like to a visiting trade delegation from Saudi Arabia. No orders are won.

The overtime budget of a shipbuilding company is already overspent. No new overtime is authorized and the ship ends up three months late to the customer. Massive penalties result.

The departmental budget in the chemistry department of a university is underspent with one month of the financial year to go. The professor authorizes a spending spree to ensure his budget is not cut next year. Unneeded equipment which is rarely if ever used is purchased.

Having a plan, which is all the budget is, can only be a good thing. In these examples, the budgets themselves were not to blame for the unfortunate results. So what went wrong?

Activity 46 · · 6 mins

Write down any ideas you have about who or what was responsible for the problems arising in any of the situations described above.

_____

_____

_____

_____

A budget is only a plan and provides guidance. Budgets should not be rigidly kept to as an excuse for not managing. Sometimes an adaptation of a plan is more sensible.

You may have noted a number of possibilities but perhaps we can narrow them down to the following.

■ An over-rigid view of how the budgets should be enforced has been taken – this seems likely to be the case in the first and second examples.
■ The budgets have been badly produced, managed and controlled, particularly the third and fourth examples.

If necessary, senior management usually have authority to over-ride a budget if they consider it would be economically worthwhile to do so. For example, it is probably appropriate to intervene to prevent the company having to pay contract penalties for late delivery, because its overtime budget is overspent. They might achieve this by transferring savings made in one budget to another, a process known as **virement**.

After all, budgets are intended to be beneficial.

It is when they are badly produced, managed and/or controlled, that they can have undesirable consequences.

But what do we mean by this? The easiest way to see how bad production, management and control of budgets have poor effects is to trace through the problems in one of the situations above.

Let's take a look at the hospital training budget example.

■ The training budget was drawn up at the beginning of the financial year without reference to the equipment budget, which showed that new equipment was being purchased to monitor heart disease.
■ BAD PRODUCTION – more access to information would have shown the need to budget for this training.

- Two key staff left and were not replaced. Instead a series of temporary staff, each of whom had to be trained in certain procedures, were taken on, so using up the training budget.
- BAD MANAGEMENT – more effort should have gone into recruiting permanent staff.
- A discretionary training course became available which had not been planned at the beginning of the year. All staff were ordered by the human resources department to go on the course, without evaluation of whether it was needed by the departments holding the training budget.
- BAD CONTROL – the usefulness of the training course in comparison with the heart disease monitor course should have been evaluated by the managers responsible for the heart disease ward.

Having seen the downside of poor practice, let us look at the benefits of good budget practice.

5 The advantages of budgets

Organizations benefit in a number of areas through budgeting.

- Co-ordination and team work

The process of budgeting means that management at all levels and in different departments are given the opportunity to meet, discuss and relate their targets to each other. Organizations are most successful if everyone works together to meet common goals rather than each manager acting selfishly to build their own empires.

The co-ordination process helps managers get an understanding of how each activity relates to the whole, which is very important for them and for the business. It would be pointless, for example, for the sales manager to plan a 10% increase if the production manager is aiming for a 5% cutback.

- Communication

In order to work to a budget, people have to **know** what is possible or impossible in their own workplace.

Budgeting encourages management at all levels to talk to one another about the company's policies and the targets they are aiming for. Again this builds team work; people working for each other and for their organizations.

■ Planning

As we've seen, planning is at the heart of a budgeting system. Using a budgeting system means that managers and supervisors have to use formal procedures to think about the future, instead of muddling along from one day to the next. It also means that thought is given to the level of performance expected in every part of the organization.

■ Control and performance evaluation

The whole point of a budget is to influence the direction the organization is taking. For a budget to be of value,

the actual outcome must be regularly compared with the planned outcome.

If the two don't match up, then controls can be used to take appropriate action. Without a plan there is no yardstick to measure what's happening; any controls, therefore, are fairly random.

The idea of a system of budgets is to get a clearer picture of planned activities and to make departments and individuals responsible for spending and cost control in their own areas. In this way, the strengths of sections and departments can be capitalized on, and ways found to overcome any weaknesses.

■ Motivation

The more people are involved at every level in setting up a budget, and in the planning and control that goes with it, the more they understand and support what the organization is trying to achieve. Involvement is an important motivating factor at any level.

All these points are valid, but the two most important purposes of budgets are **planning** and **control**. The planning process enables control to be exercised.

Let's explore the idea of budgetary control a little further.

6 Using budgetary control

Budgetary control involves drawing up budgets which relate what has to be done to the managers who have to do it, and then comparing actual results against the plan.

It is a very useful management tool. It should enable a manager or supervisor to do his or her job more effectively, without detracting from individual skill or flexibility.

Control must be an active process.

Activity 47 · 4 mins

Here is an important question for a manager, which budgets should help to provide the answer to. 'Is my work team (or section, or department) keeping its spending within agreed limits?'

Can you think of at least **one** other question to which a manager might want to know the answer, and which budgets should help provide?

_____

_____

_____

You may have thought of several possible questions. Perhaps you included the following.

- 'Are we reaching agreed targets?'
- 'If we are not reaching agreed spending limits or agreed targets, where are we falling down, and for what reasons?'
- 'What can I do to try to improve the performance of my team?'
- 'Do events suggest that the budget needs to be modified?'

By monitoring actual results against budgets, control is improved. You should be able to identify problems and take action quickly, and there is less incentive just to let matters slide.

No budget is perfect. Unforeseen circumstances do arise. For example, a competitor may suddenly bring out a new product, the bottom may drop out of a market or we may have a strike on our hands. Any number of events can make budgeted figures less accurate, some within the control of managers, some not.

Activity 48

This Activity may provide the basis of appropriate evidence for your S/NVQ portfolio. If you are intending to take this course of action, it might be better to write your answers on separate sheets of paper.

Think about your own job.

Write down **two** factors that might make your work team deviate from its budget, and which are largely **within** your control.

_____

_____

_____

_____

Now write down **two** factors that might make your work team deviate from its budget, which are largely **outside** your control.

_____

_____

_____

_____

Your response will be related to your own job.

■ As factors within your control you might have put down answers such as faulty work, bad timekeeping by employees, inefficient organization of the department, new staff not inducted properly, and so on.

■ Factors likely to be outside a line manager's control are the hold-up of supplies, teething problems with new products or systems, shortages of staff and so forth.

Because there are many ways in which a budget can become out of line with the plan, an organization must try to obtain the best possible information at the time of preparing the budget. It should look to see, for instance, what it has achieved in the past, and what its costs actually are.

Self-assessment 4

1   A properly drawn-up budget can be described as having **four** important features. Identify all four features.

_____

_____

_____

_____

2   Write down **two** initial uses for budgets at the time when they are drawn up.

_____

_____

_____

_____

3   Fill in the missing words in the following sentences.

a Budgets are largely a waste of time unless they are actively _____ in order to see whether the organization is _____ its targets and keeping within its limits.

b We use the term _____ _____ to cover the use of budgets to help an organization control its progress towards what it has set out to achieve.

c A budget will not be useful to an organization if it is managed so _____ that it does not permit some degree of flexibility.

Answers to these questions can be found on pages 122–3.

7 Summary

- A budget is a **plan**, usually described in financial terms, prepared in advance of a defined period of time.

- The starting point in producing a budget is to determine the **key** or **limiting factor** which influences all other budgets. This will often be the sales budget.

- **Control** is central to the budgeting process. The system of using budgets and comparing actual and budgeted results to control progress towards stated objectives is **budgetary control**.

- Budgeting should never be so inflexible as to prevent sensible decisions being taken.

- Budgets can also help to improve:
  - co-ordination and team work;
  - communication;
  - motivation.

- Good budgeting should help an organization meet its goals and ensure that everyone works together towards those goals.

Session E
Monitoring performance against budget

1 Introduction

Producing a correct and realistic budget takes time. Putting the information together can take you away from your main job of producing or providing a service and make you ask yourself if budgeting is really worth all the expense and effort.

We have seen the benefits, but unless budgets really work they are not worth preparing.

In this session we look at several ways in which budgets are used, and what makes them important, especially in terms of planning and control.

As a first line manager you will be involved in implementing the budget allocation of your section or department in detail. You will monitor operations and ensure that your work team works within budget as far as is possible, and will report on any differences from budget.

In this session you will see what costs you can control and which are uncontrollable. Knowing that will help you understand what actions you can take to make best use of the resources at your disposal and how to monitor those resources.

● 2 Budgetary control

All budgetary control systems follow basically the same steps:

EXTENSION 5
Further aspects of
budgetary control are
featured in *Budgeting for
Non-Financial Managers*
by Ian Maitland.

- establish agreed budgets;
- report actual results to departmental managers;
- identify where actual performance differs from planned performance (these differences are called **variances**);
- analyse which department and which manager is responsible for the variances;
- analyse why the variances have happened.

Activity 49

Acme Machine Tools Ltd prepared budgets for income from sales of machines (sales revenue) of £2,000,000 in the coming year. In the event, actual sales revenue turns out to be £1,750,000.

Identify **two** possible reasons why you think the variance (the difference between the planned and actual sales revenue) might have arisen, and who you think will be held accountable for the difference from the plan.

_____

_____

_____

You may have thought of a number of possible reasons why the variance came about, but your suggestions can probably be grouped into these main areas:

- sales price per machine had to be lower than forecast;
- the number of machines sold was fewer than forecast.

Of course, these problems would have to be investigated in more depth to find out what was causing them. It might be something like poor delivery dates, low quality or a competitor putting a better or cheaper product on the market.

As to who would be held accountable or responsible, it will be whoever was responsible for preparing the sales budget, whether that was the sales director, sales manager or whoever. This person may not be directly to blame for the variance, but he or she carries the responsibility for the problem.

Depending on the causes identified, the sales director will wish to discuss the issues with other managers. Poor delivery dates may be down to the distribution manager or the production director; low quality may also be part of the production director's remit, or that of the research and development director.

In order to monitor what is happening, managers need budgetary control reports to be sent to them periodically, highlighting variances for which they are responsible. Regular control is more likely to prevent major problems at the end of the budget period.

2.1 Reporting actual results and variances

Here is an extract from a budgetary control report for a manufacturing company.

	Budget	Actual	Variance	
Sales revenue	600,000	700,000	100,000	Favourable
Less costs:				
Materials in factory	250,000	280,000	30,000	Adverse
Wages in factory	100,000	120,000	20,000	Adverse
Machine running costs	45,000	50,000	5,000	Adverse
Salaries in administration	55,000	50,000	5,000	Favourable
General administration	20,000	15,000	5,000	Favourable
Advertising	15,000	20,000	5,000	Adverse
	485,000	535,000	50,000	Adverse
Operating profit	115,000	165,000	50,000	Favourable

As you can probably see from the figures above, a **favourable variance** indicates that:

- actual sales are greater than budgeted sales, or
- actual costs are lower than budgeted costs.

An **adverse variance** indicates that:

- actual sales are lower than budgeted sales, or
- actual costs are greater than budgeted costs.

In the example budgetary control report:

Sales − Costs = Operating profit.

You read just now that managers responsible for different budgets should periodically receive a budgetary control report, and should then be expected to explain variances. Usually senior management would be concerned with adverse variances of a certain size (some variance either way is almost inevitable), but favourable variances may also need investigation. This is because short cuts may have been taken to arrive at the apparent advantageous situation. Alternatively, managers may simply wish to learn from it for the future.

Activity 50 · 6 mins

Refer back to the budgetary control report for the manufacturing company, shown above.

Below is a list of the managers who receive a copy. Against each job title, state the variance which you think each of them would have to explain.

Purchasing manager (reports to factory manager)

_____

Factory manager

_____

Marketing manager

_____

You should have identified that the managers would have to explain the adverse variances as follows.

- Purchasing manager: materials in factory.
- Factory manager: materials and wages in factory, machine running costs.
- Marketing manager: advertising.

2.2 Why have the variances happened?

As we saw in the budget preparation statement, problems are likely to be interrelated, so that what happens in one area may be the result of a decision made in another area.

It is worth investigating the sales variance as something might be gained for other aspects of the business from the successes being achieved here. The same can also be said in the areas of salaries in administration and general administration, where the favourable variances are significant.

Managers may not always be able to take action about variances, whether favourable or adverse. This is because:

- some costs will be non-controllable;
- some costs may arise in the department but the responsibility may lie elsewhere. For example, time wasted in one department may be caused by the failure of another department to supply information or materials.

Activity 51

**S/NVQ
D6**

This Activity may provide the basis of appropriate evidence for your S/NVQ portfolio. If you are intending to take this course of action, it might be better to write your answers on separate sheets of paper.

Think about your own organization.

a To whom do you report variances from budgets and how quickly do you need to report?

_____

_____

_____

b Who, if anyone, reports variances to you?

_____

_____

_____

_____

c Why is it important for variances to be reported as required by your organization? How well are reports of variances followed up; are the causes always sought?

_____

_____

_____

_____

Your response will be related to your own job.

You are likely to report variances to your immediate line manager within a period depending on the significance of the variance. A major problem will require immediate reporting. In the same way, others may report to you.

The speed and extent of reporting depends on organizational policy and the trust you and your colleagues have in each other to deal with problems. You will presumably be able to take action on variances and take control of appropriate resources under your control, or make recommendations to your manager.

2.3 Non-controllable costs

Let's look a little more closely at what we mean by non-controllable costs. These are costs that are charged to a **budget centre**, the name given to a section of business on which a budget is built, such as sales or production, but which cannot be influenced by the actions of the people responsible for that budget centre.

Activity 52 · 2 mins

Identify **one** example of what you think is a non-controllable cost that might be charged to the budget of your work area.

_____

Here are some examples which came readily to my mind. I hope you can see that they are outside a manager's control.

- A portion of the rates charged to a departmental budget for the premises it occupies.
- Diesel fuel costs charged against the transport manager's budget where oil shortages cause prices to soar.
- Heating costs in a work area where the heating system is controlled centrally.

Since these are outside the control of the manager concerned, it's important to identify them separately. Let's look at why this is important.

Activity 53 · 6 mins

Margaret Shaw is the manager of a school canteen with a monthly wages budget of £2,000. She receives a budgetary control report which tells her that the wages expenditure in her canteen for January, February and March has been £2,250 for each month.

Here are the reasons for overspending.

- January: extra staff employed to cover sickness.
- February: staff overtime to meet re-arranged schedules during annual school examinations.
- March: implementation of a nationally agreed bonus scheme, which was not built into the budget.

We usually regard wages as a controllable cost. But is that entirely true in this case?

Decide whether the adverse variance in each month has been caused by controllable or non-controllable wages costs, and note briefly the reason for your decision.

	Controllable	Non-controllable	Reason
January	☐	☐	_____ _____
February	☐	☐	_____ _____
March	☐	☐	_____ _____

Compare your answers with mine.

- January's variance is **non-controllable**. A reasonable allowance for sickness should be built into the budget, but extra cost caused by excessive sickness could hardly be controlled by the manager.
- February's cost, however, is **controllable**. The manager should have anticipated this problem. Overtime costs for predictable events would certainly be regarded as being within the manager's control.
- March's extra costs are clearly **non-controllable**. National agreements lie outside the manager's control, and the budget will need to be adjusted to incorporate the extra payment.

We've said that it's important to discover who and what is responsible for any budget variance. This isn't a question of looking for someone to blame. The real issue is finding out why the variance has happened so that corrective action can be taken if necessary.

2.4 Causes of variances

At the beginning of this session we looked for reasons why there might be a variance on sales and decided that two of the likely causes are:

- the quantity sold is different from the quantity budgeted (volume);
- the selling price is different from the price budgeted (price).

Let's see how the variance on sales for the manufacturing company referred to on page 87 would be presented in the budgetary control report for the sales director. First we need a little more detail.

Remember that the company budgeted to make £600,000 in revenue and actually made £700,000. Why did this happen?

On investigation, we discover that the company budgeted to sell 50,000 units at £12 per unit, but actually sold 56,000 units at £12.50 per unit. How does this information help us?

We need to analyse the total sales variance into a volume variance (selling 6,000 more units than expected) and a price variance (selling units at 50p more than expected).

This can be presented as follows. (Don't worry too much about the maths at this point.)

	Budget	Actual	Variance
Sales volume	50,000 units	56,000 units	£72,000 Favourable
Selling price	£12.00	£12.50	£28,000 Favourable
Sales revenue	£600,000	£700,000	£100,000 Favourable

Having broken down the causes of the sales variance, the company needs to discover the underlying reasons.

Perhaps, in this case, the unit price was increased because another supplier went out of business and supplies were scarce, or because less discount was offered to customers. There could be all sorts of reasons.

We've seen that it's important to analyse sales variances by:

■ volume;
■ price.

We can analyse any variance on costs in a similar way.

Activity 54

2 mins

Remember our manufacturing company has an adverse variance of £30,000 on the cost of materials in the factory. Jot down the **two** headings under which you think those cost variances could be analysed.

_____

_____

You may not have used the same words as I have but anything on similar lines is acceptable.

■ Volume

Did the business need more materials than budgeted to produce the units?

■ Expenditure

Did it have to pay more for the materials than budgeted?

All types of costs can be analysed in this way but we're just going to concentrate on two:

■ labour;
■ materials.

Activity 55

8 mins

A job is budgeted to take 50 hours and the labour per hour is £6.00. The actual hours taken are 55 and the hourly rate paid is £6.20.

Calculate the labour cost variance and suggest **two** reasons which you think might have caused the variances in time and the rate.

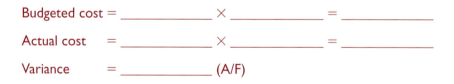

Budgeted cost = _____ × _____ = _____

Actual cost   = _____ × _____ = _____

Variance   = _____ (A/F)

Here are my calculations to compare with yours.

Budgeted cost = 50 × £6.00 = £300
Actual cost   = 55 × £6.20 = £341
Total variance = £41.00 (A)

We can break down the total variance like this.

■ For the volume variance, calculate the number of excess hours worked (55 − 50 = 5) and multiply this number by the **budgeted** hourly rate of pay (£6).

■ For the rate variance, calculate the difference between the actual rate paid and the budgeted rate (£6.20 − £6.00 = £0.20) and multiply this number by the **actual** hours paid (55).

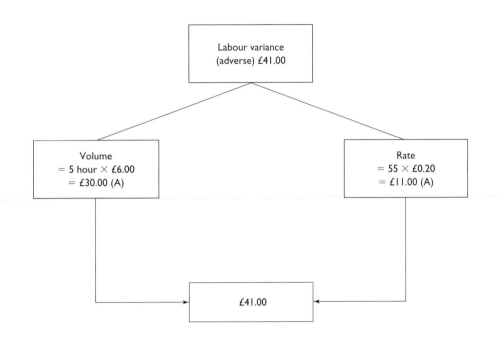

You may have suggested some of the following for the causes of the variances.

The volume variance might be caused by:

■ slack work practices resulting from poor supervision;
■ machine breakdowns;
■ technical problems;
■ bottle-necks, leading to material shortages.

The rate variance might be caused by:

■ overtime or bonus payments
■ unbudgeted pay award.

Now let's look at the cause of a total materials variance.

Activity 56 · 5 mins

A job is budgeted to use 1000 kilos of material at £3.00 per kilo.

The actual usage is 1200 kilos, but the price is £2.50 per kilo.

Calculate the total material cost variance, and analyse that into the price and expenditure variances. Write your answers on this diagram.

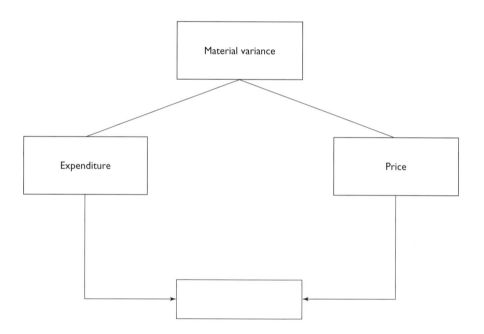

The answer to this Activity can be found on page 125.

3 Flexible budgets and budgetary control

In what we have said about budgetary control so far, we have assumed that we were using **fixed** budgets.

This means that, before the beginning of the period to which the budget relates, costs are budgeted for, and the budgeted costs remain the standard against which actual costs are compared, regardless of what happens during the budget period.

By using a **flexible budget**, on the other hand, we can make adjustments to costs if circumstances vary from the original budget.

A flexible budget is defined by the Chartered Institute of Management Accountants as:

'a budget which is designed to change in accordance with the level of activity attained'.

A flexible budget in fact consists of a series of budgets. Each one is based on a different level of sales or output. As an example, a company might budget for three possible levels of output; costs are then calculated for each level.

Despite the extra effort required in preparing these, flexible budgets can be very useful. Software packages certainly enable flexible budgets to be prepared easily and cheaply.

The first thing we have to do is to analyse costs into:

- **fixed costs**, which *do not* vary with the level of production and sales;
- **variable costs**, which *do* vary with production and sales.

Let's look at the difference this makes in practice.

We shall first assume that all costs are variable; that is, that they will vary in line with sales and production volumes. If we predict that production and sales will fall within the range of 2,000–3,000 units, we can work out the costs for both these figures.

Suppose each unit costs £5. Then the total costs for 2,000 units will be £10,000, and the total costs for 3,000 units will be £15,000.

The flexible budget would then look like this.

	Budget 1	**Budget 2**
Production/sales	2,000 units	3,000 units
Costs	£10,000	£15,000

EXTENSION 6
Managing Budgets, a title in the Essential Managers series by Dorling Kindersley, describes the usefulness of using spreadsheets in budgeting. By using spreadsheets, a change in level of activity of, say, 5% can quickly and easily be made.

In this case, the 2,000 units in Budget 1 is the lowest expected production/sales figure; the 3,000 units in Budget 2 is the highest expected figure. The actual figures are expected to fall somewhere in between these two.

Say now that actual performance is to produce and sell 2,500 units. In the budgetary control report, since sales have turned out to be within the expected range, the budget figure written in for sales will be the same as the actual figure. The actual cost can then be compared with the expected costs for that figure. In the case above, the budgetary control report might appear as follows.

	Budget	**Actual**	**Variance**
Production/sales	2,500 units	2,500 units	
Costs	£12,500	£12,000	£500 (F)

Here the actual sales turned out to be 2,500 units (which is within the budgeted range), so the 'new' expected costs are 2,500 × £5 = £12,500. The actual costs were £500 less than this, so the variance is favourable.

Of course, not all costs are in practice variable; there are always some fixed costs.

Activity 57

6 mins

Let's assume that we regard 50% of our costs as fixed and 50% as variable. The fixed costs are £5,000.

Complete the flexible budget and the budgetary control report in this instance.

Flexible budget

	Budget 1	**Budget 2**
Production/sales	2,000 units	3,000 units
Costs – fixed	£5,000	
– variable	£5,000	_____
Total costs		

Budgetary control report

	Budget	Actual	Variance
Production/sales	2,700 units	2,700 units	
Costs		£13,000	

As half the costs (£5,000) were fixed, they remain the same in Flexible Budget 2, even though sales are 1,000 more than in the first budget. But for Flexible Budget 2 we must calculate the expected variable costs for 3,000 units, as these do vary. We do this by working out the variable cost per unit from the first budget, and applying that to 3,000 units: £5,000/2,000 units = £2.50 per unit.

The variable costs for Flexible Budget 2 are then:

£2.50 × 3,000 units = £7,500.

So the total costs for Budget 2 are:

£5,000 fixed costs + £7,500 variable costs = £12,500.

The completed table is therefore as follows.

Flexible budget

	Budget 1	Budget 2
Production/sales	2,000 units	3,000 units
Costs − fixed	£5,000	£5,000
− variable	£5,000	£7,500
Total costs	£10,000	£12,500

Turning to the budgetary control report, the actual sales are 2,700 units and the actual costs are £13,000. We work out the flexible budget costs for 2,700 units as follows.

£5,000 fixed + (£2.50 × 2,700) = £11,750.

This gives an adverse variance of £1,250 (£13,000 − £11,750).
So the completed table should look like this.

Budgetary control report

	Budget	Actual	Variance
Production/sales	2,700 units	2,700 units	
Costs	£11,750	£13,000	£1,250 (A)

3.1 The advantages of flexible budgets

Flexible budgeting is helpful to management in a wide variety of organizations where it is important to be able to take account of changes in circumstances.

Flexible budgets are particularly useful at:

■ the planning stage;
■ the end of the budget period, in order to revise figures to match reality and to plan for the future.

Using flexible budgets at the planning stage lets you consider the consequences of output being greater or less than expected, within a certain range.

So, if your planned output and sales are 10,000 units, flexible budgeting will allow you to consider in advance what will be the implications of achieving only 8,000, or what will be the opportunities of achieving 12,000 units.

Activity 58

5 mins

The outpatient department of a busy district hospital plans for 25,000 outpatient visits a year. Resources – doctors, nurses, secretarial back-up, waiting rooms, etc. – are geared to cope with 25,000 visits. Management use flexible budgeting to consider in advance the problems associated with there being 20,000 or 30,000 visits.

Identify **three** problems which might be anticipated if there are as many as 30,000 visits.

_____

_____

_____

The problems may appear endless. Among these are:

■ failure to meet agreed service standards;
■ over-tired doctors and other staff;
■ overcrowding;
■ increased litigation.

A flexible budget will show what the cost implications are across the board resulting from a change, so that managers can:

- think ahead;
- anticipate problems;
- arrive at possible solutions.

4 Non-financial budgets

Let's look briefly at non-financial budgets. All the budgets we've looked at so far have been concerned with money, but we can use the same techniques to help us plan for other key factors.

Here, for example, is how they can be used to provide information for management decisions on the allocation of resources in a hospital.

Medical specialism	Beds available	Occupancy (%)
Surgery	80	75
Medical	105	80
Geriatric	110	94
Maternity	38	89
Gynaecology	20	80

Now this may not appear like a budget, but the hospital managers are:

- planning for bed usage;
- recording their resources (beds);
- recording the actual outcome (percentage occupancy);
- presumably using the information for future plans.

Activity 59 · 2 mins

Take a look at the above table.

■ Which service is most efficiently managed?

_____

■ Which service may be worth reducing?

_____

Geriatric beds are occupied 94% of the time and are used very efficiently. Compared with this, surgery beds are only 75% occupied and this may indicate that the service could be reduced.

Of course, the 'beds available figure' is just the tip of the planning iceberg. Allocating new beds implies that more nursing staff, medical staff and back-up resources will need to be allocated to the specialist areas. Percentage occupancy figures do not indicate costs.

So, you can see the budget process can help manage in a wide range of areas; it need not be restricted to financial statements.

5 Standard costing and budgetary control

Standard costing is really a continuation of budgetary control. Let's see what it is and how it relates to budgetary control.

Here is how the Chartered Institute of Management Accountants defines standard cost.

'Standard cost is a predetermined calculation of how much costs should be under specified working conditions and standard costing is therefore a system which uses standards for costs (and revenue) to allow detailed control by the use of variances.'

Using standard costs enables us to work out what performance **should** be under certain conditions, so that we can identify variances and so control actual performance.

Perhaps this sounds rather similar to what we have already said about budgeting, particularly using fixed budgets.

Both standard costing and budgeting are:

■ concerned with setting performance standards for the future;
■ aids to control.

They are not, however, the same thing.

The important difference is that:

■ budgets are concerned with totals – such as the costs of an entire department;
■ standard costs are concerned with individual units; each item of production, for instance, will have a standard cost.

Activity 60 · 2 mins

If standard costing is concerned with individual units, do you think that this involves more or fewer people in budgetary control than in budgeting? Give reasons for your answer.

_____

_____

Standard costing takes budgetary control 'further down the line', and involves more people in having responsibility for meeting standards in their particular area of work. The advantages of having people involved are:

■ if unit costs are applied widely and lots of people are monitoring them, it is possible to identify variances on a much wider range of items, so improving control;
■ the setting of standards gives everybody a target to aim for and is likely to make more people cost conscious.

Self-assessment 5

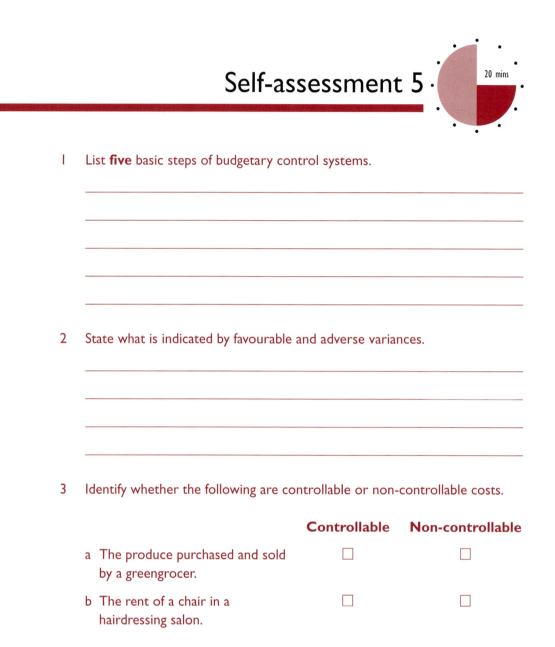

20 mins

1   List **five** basic steps of budgetary control systems.

_____

_____

_____

_____

_____

2   State what is indicated by favourable and adverse variances.

_____

_____

_____

_____

3   Identify whether the following are controllable or non-controllable costs.

	Controllable	Non-controllable
a The produce purchased and sold by a greengrocer.	☐	☐
b The rent of a chair in a hairdressing salon.	☐	☐

4   Prizewinning Blooms expects to sell 100 bunches of red roses at £8.50 per bunch on Valentine's day. Sales are hit by a newspaper promotion of chocolates and the business is only able to sell 90 bunches by reducing them to £7.00 per bunch.

Calculate the total sales variance and indicate if it is favourable or adverse.

_____

_____

_____

5   Jack Simmons has received an estimate for painting a room of £320, being 16 hours at £20. As the painter was unable to complete the job and a less qualified person completed it, the actual cost was for 24 hours at £13 per hour.

Calculate the total labour cost variance and indicate if it is favourable or adverse.

_____

_____

_____

6   Briefly explain why flexible budgeting is useful to management.

_____

_____

7   A local theatre group has fixed costs of £200. It sells tickets for £5.00 each of which £3.00 is taken up by variable costs. How many tickets must the group sell to break even?

_____

_____

Answers to these questions can be found on pages 123–4.

6 Summary

- Budgets must be put to use to achieve optimum results in organizations, in order to justify the time and effort involved in preparing them.

- Budgetary control allocates responsibility to managers who must achieve a plan, and allows for the identification and analysis of variances.

- Managers are held responsible for cost variances if these costs are within their control.

- Budgetary control can be achieved through fixed or flexible budgets, but flexible budgets are more useful.

- Non-financial budgets can provide management with useful information.

- Budgetary control is improved by a system of costing such as standard costing.

Performance checks

 1 Quick quiz

Write down your answers in the spaces below to the following questions on *Working with Costs and Budgets.*

Question 1   Complete the equation: Sales − Costs = _____

Question 2   What is meant by fixed costs?

_____

Question 3   How would you define the wages of security staff in cost terms?

_____

Question 4   Why cannot a first line manager always control costs?

_____

Question 5   Name two types of standard.

_____

Question 6   Why are variances analysed?

_____

Question 7   What is indicated by an adverse efficiency variance?

_____

Question 8   Name the two elements of standard cost.

_____

Question 9   What is a cost centre?

_____

Question 10   Briefly explain how a cost code is used.

_____

_____

_____

Question 11   Briefly explain what is meant by idle time.

_____

Question 12   Why is it important to get the work team fully involved in controlling costs?

_____

_____

Question 13   How can you maintain the interest of your work team in controlling costs?

_____

_____

Question 14   Describe what is meant by a budget.

_____

_____

Question 15   State **three** things shown by a cash budget.

_____

_____

_____

Question 16   What is likely to be the most common budget in an established business organization?

_____

Question 17   A budget is of value because it can be used to control activities. What is compared with planned outcome to achieve this?

_____

Question 18   Name an organization that uses bed occupancy as a limiting budget factor.

Question 19   What is meant by a variance?

Question 20   Briefly explain what is meant by 'non-controllable' costs.

Question 21   States of 200 units at £150 each a week are expected. In the first week, a strong demand means that 250 units are actually sold at £160 each. Calculate the sales variance and indicate whether it is favourable or adverse.

Question 22   Briefly explain the difference between fixed and variable costs.

Question 23   State the difference between budgets and standard costs.

Question 24   What should performance be compared with?

Answers to these questions can be found on pages 126–7.

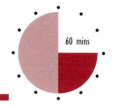

2 Workbook assessment

Read the following case incident and then deal with the questions which follow, writing your answers on a separate sheet of paper.

Pat is the catering supervisor of an organization which has decided to provide lunch for its 300 employees.

Senior managers have estimated that 80 per cent of their employees will use the restaurant for a meal on five days a week for 50 weeks in a year.

The menu, with limited choice, will be offered at a self-service counter.

An average meal is not to exceed £1.20 in materials cost to the restaurant.

The following estimates have been made.

- Gas, electricity and heating: £10,000.
- Crockery, cutlery and replacements: £2,000.
- Cleaning, laundry and sundries: £3,000.

Pat, as catering supervisor, is paid £18,000 a year.

Wages for kitchen and other staff are £5,000 a month for 12 months in a year.

1 How many meals will Pat need to provide daily?

2 What is your estimate for the number of meals per year?

3 Identify and quantify the following costs for a cost statement.

a Labour costs.
b Material costs.
c Overheads.
d Total sales required to cover the costs.
e The average selling price per meal needed to cover costs.

4   If the organization decides to charge £2 for a three-course lunch, how much is it going to have to subsidize each meal?

5   What percentage will this organizational subsidy be of the annual sales through the restaurant?

6   As catering supervisor Pat has many areas of the restaurant and kitchen to control. What are they? Explain as fully as you can what Pat will need to control and how.

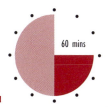

3 Work-based assignment

S/NVQ D6

The time guide for this assignment gives you an approximate idea of how long it is likely to take you to write up your findings. You will need to spend some additional time gathering information, perhaps talking to colleagues and thinking about the assignment. As you research and report, you should aim to develop your personal competency too in focusing clearly on results and influencing others with the aim of improving cost control. Ensure that you talk to people at mutually acceptable times so that the information you receive is of the best quality and that people are fully committed to helping you. You may need to convince them of the value of your work, for instance.

This Activity may provide the basis of evidence for your S/NVQ portfolio. If you are intending to take this course of action, it might be better to write your answers on separate sheets of paper.

There may be some form of cost control in your workplace. The following questions ask you to find out something about it and your role in the cost control system.

Take any product or service which your workplace is involved with and discover the following:

1   The cost of the product or service. If it is a service, explain the cost in the form of an appropriate cost unit.

2   The prime cost of the product – this is all the direct costs.

3 The overheads content of the product/service cost broken down into:

a factory or production overheads;

b administrative overheads;

c selling and distribution overheads.

4 The cost centre that you are connected to and the total cost of that cost centre for the year broken down, where appropriate, into departments and overheads.

5 The way in which the importance of cost control is communicated and how the workforce is motivated towards cost awareness. What is your role in this?

If this is not possible, use the checklists for keeping costs down to provide data for a report to your manager or trainer.

Prepare a report entitled 'Improving our control over costs' after analysing the effectiveness and relevance of present systems. Make appropriate recommendations for improvements and discuss your findings with your manager or trainer.

Reflect and review

1 Reflect and review

Now that you'll have completed your work on *Working with Costs and Budgets*, let's review our workbook objectives.

You should be better able to:

■ identify different costs and how they behave.

You have looked at direct and indirect costs, and materials, labour and general overhead costs.

■ Which types of cost are under your control? What flexibility do you have in controlling them?

_____

_____

_____

_____

Costs can be classified in order to analyse them in the workplace. This allows us to record and control costs. We have worked through costing and in doing so seen how costs occur. Everything that happens within the workplace leads to a cost in some way.

■ As a first line manager, can you clearly identify the main areas of cost in your work area and are you aware of the types of cost? Do any areas need clarifying? Make notes of any points which come to mind below.

_____

_____

_____

_____

■ Is your role in controlling costs clear, bearing in mind some areas of cost may need clarification? Are you fully in control of costs which are your responsibility? Are clarifications or changes needed?

_____

_____

_____

■ appreciate how important it is to control costs.

Fixed and variable costs are also important in organizations. It is unlikely that you can do much about fixed costs, but you can make best use of resources under your control which may be measured as variable costs.

■ Can you identify anything you can do to improve the way you manage resources under your control?

_____

_____

_____

■ understand how standard costing techniques help to control cost.

Some organizations use standard costing which can be determined as ideal, expected or current standards. If used in your organization, do you feel that they are determined and used in the best way to motivate your work team?

■ Make a note of improvements you could recommend or put into action.

_____

_____

_____

_____

Standard costs are used as a standard against which to measure our performance. Standard costing is a common way of arriving at variances from target, allowing first line managers to make adjustments and take action to keep costs down.

■ Do you feel that all standard costs identified in your work area are appropriate? Should you recommend to your manager that the standards should be altered, even if you found that standards were determined in a logical way? Why? Make a note of any changes you could propose.

_____

_____

_____

_____

■ Do you receive information about variances in a timely way? Would earlier receipt of information improve your effectiveness and how could this be achieved?

_____

_____

_____

_____

■ Use different methods for controlling and reducing costs.

To plan for the future, maintain control and measure performance we need detailed cost information. A good way of doing this is to allocate costs into cost centres against locations such as:

■ departments;
■ groups of machines;
■ individuals.

For cost centres to operate properly, first line managers need to record and communicate accurate information about the hours worked, idle time, material costs and so on.

■ Can you think of ways to improve communication in your workplace? Make a note of any suggestions you have for change below.

_____

_____

_____

■ Do you feel costs are appropriately allocated at present? Suggest changes for a fairer allocation below.

_____

_____

_____

Reflect and review

Maintaining a good cost control system takes effort and can be frustrating, especially when you are working hard to keep the costs down but still finding it difficult to keep within budget. Controlling costs is a test of leadership. You will need to be aware of cost overruns, be able to communicate problems to management and your work team, and involve your work team in keeping costs down.

■ How do you communicate the importance of controlling costs? Do you use notices and change them regularly so they are not ignored? Do you talk directly to your work team about cost control? Make a note of any improvements you feel you can make.

_____

_____

_____

_____

_____

■ Is cost control rewarded in your workplace? Should it be? Perhaps you have some thoughts you can write down now to discuss with your manager in the future.

_____

_____

_____

_____

■ Understand what a budget is and how they are used.

A budget is an expensive exercise unless it is constantly used during the period it relates to. We've seen that it can be used to compare actual performance with planned performance, and flexed to take into account changes in circumstances, or to forecast what will happen in certain circumstances and to make plans accordingly. It also helps management to set targets which ensure the profitability of the organization.

■ Can you think of ways to improve the way budgets are used in your workplace? Make a note of any suggestions you have for change.

_____

_____

_____

■ Are any budgets you use at work flexed to an appropriate extent? Write down your thoughts for future discussions with your manager.

_____

_____

_____

■ Help to draw up workable budgets.

Budgets are a way of bringing together all an organization's plans and presenting them in a way that allows people to monitor their progress against them. As a first line manager you will be involved both in generating information for budget preparation and in ensuring that variances from budget are monitored and acted upon.

How are budgets prepared in your workplace? Is the sequence correct – is the budget that contains the limiting factor prepared first, and then communicated widely? Make notes of any areas in which you feel that the sequence or communication of budgeting is inadequate, and make suggestions for improvements.

_____

_____

_____

Are you involved in collecting information for the preparation of budgets? Is the information you collect actually used? What other items of information do you think would be useful? Are your budgets up to date? Make notes on any areas of your work where out-of-date budget information has presented you with difficulties.

_____

_____

_____

■ Use some budgetary control techniques.

Looking at fairly simple examples, we've used some budgetary control techniques which would be used in your workplace. These include flexible budgeting and standard costing. If you are involved in setting the budget in your work area or are on a budget committee, the work you have done in this workbook should have increased the confidence with which you handle the techniques.

■ Make a note of techniques you could use in assisting your planning and control.

_____

_____

_____

_____

_____

2 Action plan

Use this plan to further develop for yourself a course of action you want to take. Make a note in the left-hand column of the issues or problems you want to tackle, and then decide what you intend to do, and make a note in column 2.

The resources you need might include time, materials, information or money. You may need to negotiate for some of them, but they could be something easily acquired, like half an hour of somebody's time, or a chapter of a book. Put whatever you need in column 3. No plan means anything without a timescale, so put a realistic target completion date in column 4.

Finally, describe the outcome you want to achieve as a result of this plan, whether it is for your own benefit or advancement, or a more efficient way of doing things.

Desired outcomes			
1 Issues	2 Action	3 Resources	4 Target completion
Actual outcomes			

3 Extensions

Extension 1	Book	*Simple and Practical Costing, Pricing and Credit Control*
	Author	Keith Kirkland and Stuart Howard
	Edition	First edition, 1998
	Publisher	Kogan Page

Extension 2	Book	*Financial Planning using Spreadsheets*
	Author	Sue Nugus
	Edition	First edition, 1997
	Publisher	Kogan Page

Extension 3	Book	*Cost Control: A Strategic Guide*
	Author	David Doyle
	Edition	First edition, 1994
	Publisher	Kogan Page

Extension 4	Book	*The Business Plan Workbook*
	Authors	Colin Barrow, Paul Barrow and Robert Brown
	Edition	Fourth edition, revised 2001
	Publisher	Kogan Page

Extension 5	Book	*Budgeting for Non-Financial Managers*
	Author	Ian Maitland
	Edition	1999
	Publisher	Financial Times Prentice Hall 1999

Extension 6	Book	*Managing Budgets: Essential Managers Series*
	Edition	2000
	Publisher	Dorling Kindersley

These extensions can be taken up via your ILM Centre. They will either have them or will arrange that you have access to them. However, it may be more convenient to check out the materials with your personnel or training people at work – they may well give you access. There are good reasons for approaching your own people; for example, they will become aware of your interest and you can involve them in your development.

4 Answers to self-assessment questions

Self-assessment 1 on pages 16–17

1 Direct materials costs can be identified directly and in total with an item being produced, whereas indirect materials costs have a more general use in an organization and cannot be identified directly and in total.

2 As reporters have a regular wage and advertising staff receive commission:

- the wages of the advertising staff are VARIABLE COSTS;
- the wages of the reporters are FIXED COSTS.

3 a Direct labour cost CAN be TOTALLY identified with a particular product.
 b Wages which CANNOT be identified with a particular product are INDIRECT labour costs.
 c Direct labour costs are often VARIABLE costs because they increase or decrease in proportion to the production being carried out.

4 The break-even number of members is £18,000/£15 = 1,200 members.

5 The wastage of components used in the production of hard disks should be under Sam's control. Sam is not likely to be involved in marketing and sales so advertising is not controllable by Sam, nor is Sam's basic salary which would be set by senior managers.

Self-assessment 2 on page 32

1 (a) A standard cost is a PREDETERMINED cost that is achieved by setting STANDARDS related to particular circumstances or conditions of work.

2 The two reasons for setting performance standards in any organization are:

- to base costs upon them;
- to measure actual performance.

3 The standard cost of a vase is £2.50, calculated as follows:

> **Standard cost sheet**
>
> Direct materials: £8.00 ÷ 4 = £2.00
> Direct wages: £7.50 ÷ 10 = £0.75
>   £2.75

4 Direct material cost variances comprise a usage variance and a price variance. Direct labour cost variances comprise an efficiency variance, an idle time variance and a rate variance.

5 A favourable variance indicates that actual costs are less than standard costs. An adverse variance indicates that actual costs are greater than standard costs.

Self-assessment 3 on page 68

1 a The components of prime cost are direct materials and direct labour.
   b Factory overheads are added to prime cost to arrive at the total factory cost.

2 A cost centre is a location where costs can be identified, grouped together and then finally related to a cost unit.

3 A good cost system enables costs to be:

- collected;
- analysed;
- controlled.

4 The three keys to success are:

- Involvement;
- Communication;
- Feedback.

5 Workers should be provided with information in a form they can relate to and at a time and place where the cost is incurred.

6 A checklist helps to channel thoughts and avoids the possibility of overlooking matters.

Self-assessment 4 on page 83

1 The four features of a budget are that it:
- is quantitative;
- is prepared in advance;
- relates to a particular period;
- is a plan of action.

2 Budgets are essential for deciding at the outset whether an objective can be achieved and what actions this requires. They also give managers their targets and cost limits for the next period.

3 a Budgets are largely a waste of time unless they are actively USED in order to see whether the organization is MEETING its targets and keeping within its limits.

   This helps to ensure that expenditure takes place according to plan.

   b We use the term BUDGETARY CONTROL to cover the use of budgets to help an organization control its progress towards what it has set out to achieve.

Setting targets and encouraging people to adhere to them assists the organization through a disciplined approach.

c A budget will not be useful to an organization if it is managed so RIGIDLY that it does not permit some degree of flexibility.

Unless allowances are made for changes in circumstances, organizations can incur expenses and losses in trying to achieve the impossible.

Self-assessment 5 on pages 104–5

1 The five basic steps of budgetary control systems are to:

- establish agreed budgets;
- report actual results to departmental managers;
- identify where actual performance differs from planned performance using variances;
- agree which department or who is responsible for variances;
- analyse why variances have happened.

2 A favourable variance indicates that actual sales are greater than budgeted sales, or actual costs are less than budgeted costs.

An adverse variance indicates that actual sales are less than budgeted sales, or actual costs are greater than budgeted costs.

3 a The goods purchased and sold by a greengrocer are controllable costs.

b The rent of a chair in a hairdressing salon is non-controllable.

4 The sales variance is calculated as follows.

Budgeted sales revenue	100 × £8.50 = £850	
Actual sales revenue	90 × £7.00 = £630	
Total sales variance		£220 adverse

(You could analyse the total sales variance as follows.

Volume	10 × £8.50	£85.00	adverse
Price	90 × £1.50	£135.00	adverse
Total		£220.00	adverse)

5 The labour cost variance is:

Budgeted cost	16 × £20.00 = £320	
Actual cost	24 × £13.00 = £312	
Variance		£8 favourable

(You could analyse the total labour variance as follows.

Volume	8 × £20.00	£160.00	adverse
Price	24 × £7.00	£168.00	favourable
Total		£8.00	favourable)

6   Flexible budgeting provides the opportunity to be able to take account of changes in circumstances and more closely monitor the position than is possible using fixed budgets.

7   The break-even number of tickets to be sold is calculated as:

Sales price	£5.00
Variable costs	£3.00
Contribution per ticket	£2.00

Break-even point = £200.00 ÷ £2.00 = 100 tickets

5 Answers to activities

Activity 15 on pages 24–5

Here are my completed calculations to compare with yours.

Standard cost sheet

Direct materials: 5 metres at £6.10	£30.50
Direct wages:	
Moulder 1½ hours × £8.00	£12.00
Cutter 2½ hours × £10.00	£25.00
	£67.50

So the standard cost of a table is £67.50.

Activity 24 on page 43

Since some of our codes provide a group of numbers, your suggested cost codes may not be exactly the same as mine, but I hope you can see how cost codes are actually made up.

Here are the numbers I would use:

- Theatre 1 staff nurse's salary: 098 026
- Theatre 2 medical equipment: 099 400 (or any number to 449)
- Physiotherapy department medical equipment: 264 400
- Drug coded 459 and ordered for the pharmacy: 171 459
- Canteen cook's wages: 400 197

Activity 28 on page 48

I hope we can agree on the following figures:

Regular time 40 hours at £6.00	240.00
Overtime premium 3 hours at £9.00	27.00
Gross pay for week	£267.00

Activity 56 on page 96

Budgeted material cost = 1,000 kilos × £3.00 = £3,000.
Actual material cost = 1,200 kilos × £2.50 = £3,000.
Variance = nil

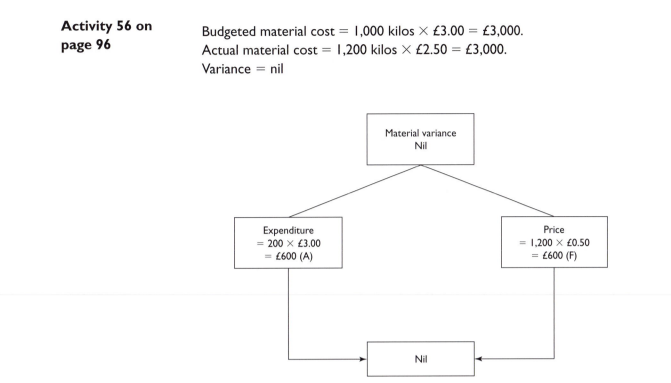

In this case, the lower price exactly counters the extra cost from using 200 kilos more than were budgeted for.

6 Answers to the quick quiz

Answer 1   Sales − Costs = profit

Answer 2   Fixed costs are costs incurred whether anything is being produced or not.

Answer 3   As an indirect labour cost or overhead.

Answer 4   Some costs are incurred by the organization as a whole.

Answer 5   Ideal, expected or current standards.

Answer 6   To aid control and planning.

Answer 7   The work team spent longer making the product than the standard indicated.

Answer 8   Costs and performance levels.

Answer 9   A location into which direct costs and overheads are gathered.

Answer 10   A cost code identifies particular types of cost and assists in analysis of the extent of these costs used in particular centres and throughout the organization.

Answer 11   Idle time is unproductive time − not spent on actual production.

Answer 12   Costs can only be controlled if the work team is committed.

Answer 13   Through communication and feedback.

Answer 14   A budget is a quantitative plan of action prepared in advance of a defined period of time.

Answer 15　　A cash budget shows:

- the cash received and paid out during the budget period;
- the timing of receipts and payments;
- the bank balance or overdraft at the end of each month.

Answer 16　　The sales budget.

Answer 17　　Actual outcome.

Answer 18　　A hotel or hospital.

Answer 19　　The difference between actual and planned performance.

Answer 20　　Costs charged to a budget centre, but which cannot be influenced by the activities of people responsible for that budget centre.

Answer 21　　Budgeted sales revenue　200 × £150 = £30,000
Actual sales revenue　　250 × £160 = £40,000
Sales variance　　　　　　　　　　£10,000 favourable

Answer 22　　Fixed costs do not vary with sales and production. Variable costs do vary.

Answer 23　　Budgets are concerned with totals whereas standard costs are concerned with individual units.

Answer 24　　Performance should be compared with past performance, desired future performance or the performance of something else.

7 Certificate

Completion of this certificate by an authorized person shows that you have worked through all the parts of this workbook and satisfactorily completed the assessments. The certificate provides a record of what you have done that may be used for exemptions or as evidence of prior learning against other nationally certificated qualifications.

superseries

Working with Costs and Budgets

....

has satisfactorily completed this workbook

Name of signatory ....

Position ....

Signature ....

Date ....

Official stamp

Pergamon
Flexible
Learning

Fifth Edition

superseries

FIFTH EDITION

Workbooks in the series:

Achieving Objectives Through Time Management	978-0-08-046415-2
Building the Team	978-0-08-046412-1
Coaching and Training your Work Team	978-0-08-046418-3
Communicating One-to-One at Work	978-0-08-046438-1
Developing Yourself and Others	978-0-08-046414-5
Effective Meetings for Managers	978-0-08-046439-8
Giving Briefings and Making Presentations in the Workplace	978-0-08-046436-7
Influencing Others at Work	978-0-08-046435-0
Introduction to Leadership	978-0-08-046411-4
Managing Conflict in the Workplace	978-0-08-046416-9
Managing Creativity and Innovation in the Workplace	978-0-08-046441-1
Managing Customer Service	978-0-08-046419-0
Managing Health and Safety at Work	978-0-08-046426-8
Managing Performance	978-0-08-046429-9
Managing Projects	978-0-08-046425-1
Managing Stress in the Workplace	978-0-08-046417-6
Managing the Effective Use of Equipment	978-0-08-046432-9
Managing the Efficient Use of Materials	978-0-08-046431-2
Managing the Employment Relationship	978-0-08-046443-5
Marketing for Managers	978-0-08-046974-4
Motivating to Perform in the Workplace	978-0-08-046413-8
Obtaining Information for Effective Management	978-0-08-046434-3
Organizing and Delegating	978-0-08-046422-0
Planning Change in the Workplace	978-0-08-046444-2
Planning to Work Efficiently	978-0-08-046421-3
Providing Quality to Customers	978-0-08-046420-6
Recruiting, Selecting and Inducting New Staff in the Workplace	978-0-08-046442-8
Solving Problems and Making Decisions	978-0-08-046423-7
Understanding Change in the Workplace	978-0-08-046424-4
Understanding Culture and Ethics in Organizations	978-0-08-046428-2
Understanding Organizations in their Context	978-0-08-046427-5
Understanding the Communication Process in the Workplace	978-0-08-046433-6
Understanding Workplace Information Systems	978-0-08-046440-4
Working with Costs and Budgets	978-0-08-046430-5
Writing for Business	978-0-08-046437-4

For prices and availability please telephone our order helpline +44 (0) 1865 474010
or email directorders@elsevier.com